BOOMERANGS ON THE FRONT COVER
in clockwise sequence, starting at upper right.

1. Concept 90 by Rusty Harding, Tennessee. Made from two pieces of red oak stuck one on top of the other! Wingspan 422mm, weight 70 grams, range about 20 metres.

2. Seagull by Sam Blight, Western Australia. Wings extend radially outward from centre of rotation. Wingspan 398mm, weight 61 grams, range about 40 metres.

3. Turning Point boomerang by Eric Darnell, Vermont. Moulded from polypropylene. Wingspan 347mm, weight 58 grams, range about 30 metres.

4. Three Sigma boomerang by John Mauro, Virginia. The prototype for the plan in chapter 9. Wingspan 388mm, wight 60 grams, range about 27 metres.

5. Long distance boomerang by Bob Burwell, Queensland. Made of fibreglass and successfully used many times in international events. Wingspan 312mm, weight 145 grams, range 111 metres.

6. Queen of Hearts by Rod Jones, Queensland. Wingspan 295mm, weight 30 grams, range about 25 metres.

7. V-shape boomerang by George Reitbauer, Pennsylvania. Intrically constructed from various woods. Wingspan 307mm, weight 58 grams, range about 30 metres.

8. V-shape boomerang by Ted Bailey, Ohio. Not a drop of stain or paint was used: the coloured patterns are due solely to inlaid natural woods. Wingspan 307mm, weight 58 grams, range about 30 metres.

9. Koala Cub polypropylene boomerang by Lorin Hawes. Wingspan 300mm, weight 35 grams, range about 20 metres.

All About the Authors

Lorin Hawes started out in 1953 as a plutonium metallurgist at Los Alamos Scientific Laboratories where he was co-discoverer of the delta-prime allotrope of plutonium metal. Allowed to serve in the U.S. Army against his expressed desires otherwise, he was assigned to Sandia Base as an instructor in nuclear weapons.

Disillusioned and fearful of the United States military programme, he emigrated to Australia in 1956 where he lectured in Chemistry and Crystallography at various universities and colleges.

He made his first boomerang in 1959, became a naturalized Australian in 1960 and left academic life in Canberra in 1965 to establish a boomerang factory and theme park in Southern Queensland.

Namer of the dingle arm and probably the first person to throw a boomerang by what others called the "wrong end" he compounded his heresy by inventing the "elbow throw" and by writing a book about boomerangs. He sold the business and retired in 1980 but, like a good boomerang, he returned. His new enterprise on Hope Island comprises a boomerang factory and theme park (not bigger and better than before, but smaller and worse) and a rookery for breeding of the Queensland cane toad.

JOHN B. MAURO

John B. Mauro showed an early interest in aerodynamics and flight by serving as a Marine Corps aerial gunner in World War II: after the war he took night college courses in aeronautical engineering while working for a New York newspaper.

He has spent most of his working life in the field of marketing research and newspapers, and discovered boomerangs in 1979.

He has combined his interests in computers and boomerangs by using mathematical curves as the basis for boomerang shapes. He joined the United States Boomerang Association at an early stage and has written and published a booklet AN INTRODUCTION TO BOOMERANGS. John was captain of the United States Boomerang Team and is a past president of the United States Boomerang Association.

LORIN HAWES

ALL ABOUT
boomerangs

LORIN LINDLEY HAWES

AND

JOHN BAPTIST MAURO

Illustrated by
ROD SCOTT and DONNA PINNIX

Published by HAWES BOOMERANGS
3 Goroka Place, Runaway Bay, Queensland 4216
First published in 1967
© 1967, 1975, 1987 by Sir Lorin Lindley Hawes
Produced in Australia by the Publisher
Printed by Jon the Printer, 7 United Road,
Ashmore, Gold Coast, Queensland 4214
ISBN 0 600 073777

ACKNOWLEDGEMENTS

Special thanks are due to the Department of Anthropology of the Museum of Western Australia and to David R. Moore, Curator of Anthropology at the Australian Museum, Sydney, for kind permission to examine and photograph collections of rare Australian Aboriginal boomerangs. Thanks are also due to the Trustees of the Mitchell Archives of the Library of New South Wales for permission to examine early manuscript journals on the exploration of Australia.

Many of the thoughts presented in this book were formulated and crystallized as the result of correspondence over the course of years — With Dr. Peter Musgrove, Dr. Felix Hess, Ben Ruhe and Rusty Harding, and with personal discussions with Bill Onus, Frank Donnellan, Neville Bonner, Cecil Burwell and Harold Blair.

Thanks are due to Richard (Boomerang Man) Harrison, doubtless the world's leading enthusiast and dealer, for sending me newer type boomerangs from time to time, and for his kind permission to reproduce his copyrighted koala bear cartoon.

And the warmest, most genuine and profuse thanks must go to Mr. Stephen Silady of Sydney for his enthusiastic criticism and rubbishing of the second edition of this book. Were it not for this, nobody would ever have heard of it and it probably wouldn't have sold more than a dozen copies!

PREFACE TO THE THIRD EDITION

ALL ABOUT BOOMERANGS first appeared in 1967 — a small booklet of information about boomerangs: how to make them, how to throw them under various conditions, facts and fallacies about them.

A short time later, with permission, the booklet was adopted by the Smithsonian Institution of Washington, D.C. along with other material by the author as the basis for a course of instruction on boomerangs.

The popularity of this course over a number of years thus gave a wider dissemination to the material than was originally envisaged, and contributed significantly to the growing popularity of boomerang throwing around the world.

With the helpful urging of Ben Ruhe, then director of the Smithsonian boomerang programme, an expanded hardback edition was published in 1975 for commercial distribution. It was greeted with surprise, scepticism and worldwide publicity, largely because of statements in it which appeared heretical for the day — that boomerangs and similar throwing sticks were not unique to Australia — that the boomerang itself was not a hunting weapon designed to give the thrower a second chance if it missed its quarry initially.

The worldwide distribution of the English and French versions of ALL ABOUT BOOMERANGS helped foster a degree of awareness of the fun of boomerang throwing and soon there were groups of enthusiasts, clubs, and national bodies everywhere enjoying this fascinating pastime.

The boomerang has changed more since 1967 than it did during its previous history, and to this extent some of the incidental material in previous editions became outdated: ALL ABOUT BOOMERANGS was becoming a victim of the tide that it, as the first book on boomerangs, had helped to generate! For example — previously it had been stated in good faith that all boomerangs stayed in the air about the same time — eight to twelve seconds. But this was before the inspired efforts of Ted Bailey which revolutionized the topic: now the best throws stay up about three minutes!

And my own record of two minutes, nine seconds for ten throws and catches in the Australian National championships in 1973 looks fairly pathetic compared with 18.7 seconds for five throws and catches, the current record.

More pictures of boomerangs have been added in this edition to illustrate the amazing variety of shapes now current, as well as the contents of my throwing bag, shown on the covers. Of the modern style boomerangs in my collection, one in particular has always stood out as being extremely good. Even when I knew I had thrown it badly it always seemed to come back somehow and hover around long enough to be caught. It was the THREE SIGMA boomerang designed and made by John Mauro, genial past president of the U.S. Boomerang Association and former captain of the U.S. Boomerang Team.

Thus, when he wrote to me some months ago to suggest that I should arrange to reprint ALL ABOUT BOOMERANGS I had no hesitation in agreeing that it was an excellent idea — if he would contribute his thoughts toward updating it — and allow the inclusion of plans for his THREE SIGMA boomerang. Happily, he agreed.

The result is in your hands.

LORIN HAWES
3 Goroka Place,
Runaway Bay,
Queensland 4216.

November, 1987.

CONTENTS

NOTE: Pages of boomerang pictures are scattered throughout the book and are not listed above. In the cases of early Aboriginal types, both boomerangs and kylies are illustrated with an admitted bias toward those which appear capable of a returning flight. Due to the vigilance of museum authorities, flight testing was not possible with any of these.

1.
FACTS AND FALLACIES

'Alas! Thou hast misconstrued everything.'
Julius Caesar. V iii

About ninety per cent of all that has been written about boomerangs is sheer bunk, and most of the commonly accepted knowledge about the subject is not only erroneous but preposterous as well. This is perhaps to be expected, for the very idea of throwing a stick away and having it come back does seem a bit far fetched.

To set the record straight, let us examine briefly some of the fallacies which have become so widely established that they are usually accepted unquestioningly. In later chapters some of these fallacies will be re-examined in closer detail.

Fallacy: The boomerang was intended originally for hunting, so that if it missed the kangaroo at which it was aimed, it would return so that the hunter could try again.

Fact: Boomerangs were never intended for use as weapons, for they must be very light in order to return—too light to do any real damage to anything big enough to make a decent meal for a hungry Aborigine.

Fallacy: It is remarkable that primitive people were able to work out the complex aerodynamics and physics of the boomerang in the days before computers.

Fact: It is not necessary to understand how something works in order to apply it. What **is** remarkable about the matter is that while that great genius Leonardo da Vinci was filling reams of paper with sketches of helicopters that were never built and which wouldn't have worked anyway, thousands of Australian Aborigines were enjoying themselves with working models of this principle, which they had discovered independently through practical rather than theoretical knowledge.

Fallacy: The Aborigines used two kinds of boomerangs, the returning type and the non-returning type.

Fact: The Aborigines used 'killer sticks' or **kylies** for hunting, and boomerangs for recreation and for developing throwing skills in the young. The distinction is subtle but straightforward: a boomerang is not a boomerang unless it boomerangs!

Fallacy: Boomerangs made by the old-time Aborigines were far better than those made today, and making them has become a lost art.

Fact: This is partly true. Most 'boomerangs' sold in Australia and elsewhere are incapable of returning (though no salesperson will admit it), although nearly all of them come with a sheet of so-called 'throwing instructions'. However, when properly applied, modern materials and aerodynamic know-how can produce boomerangs whose flight paths leave the 'old originals' for dead. Because of the poor materials at hand, and the lack of precision power tools, it was a real challenge for the Aboriginal boomerang-making pioneers to achieve a returning flight. Generally, the older boomerangs in use about the time Australia was settled by the British were far too heavy for optimum efficiency, were hard to throw, and were unspectacular in performance compared with modern boomerangs.

Let it not be forgotten that the Wright brothers' original aeroplane would not compare too favourably with a modern aircraft. It was highly significant, nonetheless, just as the original boomerangs were uniquely important as man's first application of the helicopter principle.

Fallacy: The 'old original' boomerangs were highly decorated with animal and bird carvings or paintings.

Fact: They were usually plain and undecorated with, at most, a little ochre daubed on in the form of stripes or zigzags. The carved and otherwise decorated ones which are seen in profusion today, and which are peddled in large numbers in various souvenir stores, are made that way because they are the ones that the majority of souvenir buyers want. Traditional Australian scenes carved or painted on boomerangs (kangaroos, koala bears, the Sydney Harbour Bridge with the Opera House in the background) are a tribute to the lack of taste of today's buying public rather than an accurate reflection of traditional Aboriginal lore.

Fallacy: Bent branches or roots from trees are the best materials from which to make boomerangs.

Fact: They are among the worst, being inherently weak along the grain and tending to split when they hit something hard. Even worse, sections of bent wood tend to warp badly with changes in humidity, so that a boomerang may become unthrowable after a time even if it was properly made initially.

Fallacy: The two arms of a boomerang are identical, and in perfect balance.

Fact: On the best and most accurate boomerangs, not only are the arms contoured differently, but they are of differing lengths and weights as well. While a boomerang may not appear to be in balance when held at its midpoint on top of a finger, it automatically balances itself dynamically in flight.

Fallacy: There is no such thing as a left-handed boomerang any more than there is a left-handed screwdriver or wrench.

Fact: There sure is. Any object that looks different from its reflection in a mirror can have right and left-handed versions, and a boomerang, like a golf club, falls into this category (while knives, forks and screwdrivers do not.) This is very important if you are left-handed, for you will require a special boomerang that your right-handed friends will be unable to throw in a normal way. It goes round in a clockwise path and is the mirror image of a right-handed boomerang.

Fallacy: Throwing a boomerang is fairly difficult and requires great skill and much practice.

Fact: There are many wrong ways to throw a boomerang, and plenty of 'boomerangs' on the market that won't come back. But with a good boomerang and instructions, anyone over the age of seven should be able to get the thing to come back within a few throws.

Fallacy: When throwing a boomerang, it should be held with the concave edge forward—like a sickle.

Fact: It doesn't make a great deal of difference which **end** is held so long as the boomerang is inclined at the correct angle, with the flat side outward, and spins fast. After it has left the hand, the boomerang has no way of remembering at which end it was held.

Fallacy: There is a special 'flick of the wrist' that gives the boomerang its spin.

Fact: The motion of the wrist during a throw is actually very slight. Most of the spin is imparted to the boomerang by bending and locking the index finger around the tip of the boomerang, which thus has to pivot sharply around the finger in order to leave the hand, acquiring a fast spin in the process.

Fallacy: Boomerangs should be thrown so as to leave the hand spinning in a horizontal plane.

Fact: This is the worst possible way to throw a boomerang. It will swoop straight up into the sky and may then come straight down, hitting the ground with a tragic splintering sound. The boomerang should instead be held at an angle of about 30 degrees from the vertical so as to fly a level course.

Fallacy: There must be a breeze into which the boomerang is thrown.

Fact: Wind is not necessary or even desirable for the flight of a true returning boomerang. Even a light breeze of five kilometres per hour makes it difficult for the thrower to achieve any degree of accuracy. Bad boomerangs, however, will often only come back if thrown into a fairly stiff breeze so that the wind essentially blows the boomerang to return (as would a bunch of grapes, for that matter), but this isn't what the sport of boomerang throwing is all about.

Early Boomerangs
From the Australian Museum, Sydney.

1 From the Captain Cook collection. Probably the first souvenir of Australia to be seen by the outside world, and most likely the oldest complete Australian boomerang or kylie in existence.
Weight: 300 grams.

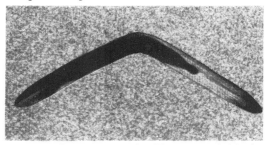

2 From Central Australia. Has pointed, blackened ends, and is made from mulga.
Weight: 155 grams.

3 From Western Australia. Notably thin in cross section.
Weight: 130 grams.

4 From Ipswich, Queensland, a region noted for excellent true boomerangs.
Weight: 200 grams.

10.

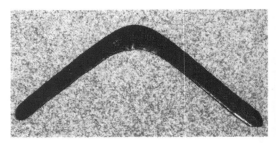

5 From Daly River district, Northern Territory. Has pointed tips and is left-handed.
Weight: 240 grams.

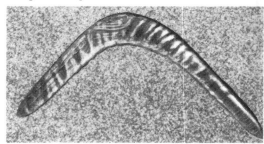

6 From South Australia. Smeared with brown and red ochre, and is left-handed.
Weight: 150 grams.

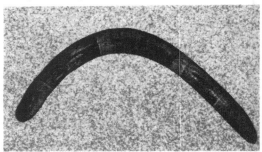

7 An early 'hook' boomerang, location unknown.
Weight: 175 grams.

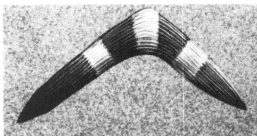

8 Deeply incised striations, sharply pointed tips, with red and white ochre stripes.
Weight: 108 grams.

2.
BOOMERANGS AND RELATED THROWING STICKS IN HISTORY

'I should not waste a word on these unexplained oddities if they only existed in one place in the world. But they are found almost everywhere.'
Erich von Daniken: *Chariots of the Gods*

It comes as a surprise to many people to learn that boomerangs and similar throwing sticks have been found in locations as varied as India, Egypt, the New Hebrides, Holland, Denmark, Germany, Sudan, Arizona, Jutland and Tasmania, as well as on the Australian mainland continent.

Boomerangs reached their greatest stage of development in Australia, where they remained in common use into modern times. In other parts of the world (with the exception of Arizona) they had pretty well faded from the scene many hundreds of years ago, having become obsolete with the invention of the bow and arrow.

The origins of the boomerang are obscure, for its invention occurred in prehistoric times. A theory such as the one which follows is therefore conjectural and subject to modification should archeological discoveries shed more light on the subject—but, barring this, here is how the boomerang probably evolved:

People in a primitive hunting society are keenly involved with the relative merits and shortcomings of weapons used in acquiring game and in anything that will extend the range or improve the accuracy of these weapons. The various missiles which were used in hunting—rocks, spears, sticks—are all affected to about the same extent by the relentless pull of gravity, and fall to earth at the rapidly increasing rate of 4.8 metres in the first second, 14.6 metres in the next, and so forth. As teachers of physics point out, after a few seconds a freely falling body is falling very fast indeed.

This makes it difficult for a hunter unless his quarry is fairly close by, for it means that he must aim his missile progressively higher and must throw it very strongly to have any chance of scoring a hit—until finally he is aiming upward at an angle of 45 degrees and throwing with all of his strength. Clearly, this does not make for accuracy.

A spinning bent stick which is approximately flat on the bottom and curved on the top is a different proposition. Its overall flat configuration means that it can skim through the air. If it has an appropriate twist at the centre, or cutaway portions on the underside of one or both arms, it becomes a rotating wing capable of keeping itself aloft by aerodynamic lift rather than by being propelled upward. It thus frees itself, for a while at least, from the gravitational acceleration which plunges other missiles into the ground.

This is accomplished at the constant expense of a small portion of the energy acquired in spinning, but this is inconsequential since a spinning bent stick packs a terrific punch on impact compared with a straight stick that is not spinning—a punch more than enough to stun a kangaroo, emu or goanna.

This type of 'killer stick' is commonly called a **kylie** by the Australian Aborigines, who still use it, and has a range very much greater than a thrown stone or spear.

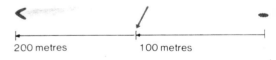

200 metres   100 metres

Fig. 1

Throws of about 200 metres across flat open ground are commonly achieved by these nomadic hunters—and it's easy to get within that distance of a kangaroo.

The fact that a kylie spins, and also covers a swath almost a metre wide, adds to its desirability as a weapon, since this allows a greater margin of error than does a rock or spear. All in all, the kylie is a very sophisticated and effective weapon, and it isn't surprising that it was used in all inhabited areas of the Australian continent.

The kylie does not fly in a straight line. Each one swerves in its own peculiar way, and its user must be familiar with it and adjust his throw accordingly if he is to hit the target. It is likely that some adventurous soul, many years ago, discovered through trial-and-error which wing surfaces influenced this swerving. By accentuating certain wing surfaces, and by greatly reducing the weight, he (or probably they) eventually developed the boomerang or 'come back stick'.

The true boomerang never enjoyed the widespread distribution enjoyed by killer sticks, being common only in the eastern part of Australia where it was used chiefly for sport and for developing the throwing skills of the young. Boomerangs were forbidden to women, probably for religious reasons, but this was of little consequence due to the inherent ineptness of the gentler sex, even to this day, in operating the things successfully.

It was implied earlier that the boomerang was not used in hunting. While this is generally true, there are records of its being thrown to hover near one end of a flock of birds resting on the water while the thrower made hawk-like cries. This caused the flock to take off in panic, away from the boomerang, towards the rest of the hunting party waiting with nets and sticks.

In view of the popularity of boomerangs and kylies in prehistoric Australia it is paradoxical that the oldest and best preserved specimens are those from other lands, particularly Egypt and northern Europe. In Australia, presumably, these implements were either lost in the open where they weathered away, or were used until they broke and then burned as fuel.

In Egypt, on the other hand, boomerangs were more highly regarded. They were often enclosed in tombs with other items designed to make life in the spirit world more pleasant for the departed. Boomerangs in excellent condition were found in the tomb of Tutankhamun (1371-1352 BC). Many of these had ends capped with gold, presumably to increase their range and retention of spin.

Boomerangs from northern Europe owe their excellent preservation to being lost in peat bogs and hence protected from weathering and oxidation. It is likely that the oldest boomerang in existence is one made of oak, recently unearthed in Holland after having been lost for thousands of years.

Not much is known today of the flight characteristics of any of the early boomerangs or kylies—museum curators are understandably reluctant to allow them to be thrown. Some reproductions, accurate in contours and weight, have been made and by throwing these replicas it has been established that the ancient Dutch boomerang, and at least one specimen from Egypt, were true returning boomerangs.

The discoverers and early explorers of the Australian continent did not appreciate the function or the aerodynamic nature of

The 'Captain Cook boomerang', weighing 300 grams, is probably a non-returning killer stick rather than a returning boomerang. Museum authorities are understandably reluctant to lend it for a proving flight.

Fig. 2

boomerangs and kylies. They were basically different from anything in use in Europe at the time, and for fifty years after the landing of Captain Cook it was assumed that these implements were swords and scimitars — and they were described as such in the early journals of exploration.

Captain Cook had the distinction of being the first tourist to return home with a throwing stick as a souvenir of Australia. The magnificent kylie he acquired later made a 'return trip' to Australia where it is now preserved in the vaults of the Australian Museum in Sydney

For generations of Australians, a boomerang should look like what was shown on the old £5 note... otherwise it's regarded with suspicion. In this continent, the spiritual home of the boomerang, the various modern shapes aren't accepted by the public.

3.
WHAT A BOOMERANG IS...
AND WHY IT COMES BACK

'I shall return.'
Douglas MacArthur

LORIN HAWES

In an intelligent discussion about any subject, a good starting point is defining the subject—and in few cases is this more difficult than with a boomerang. There is simply no consensus of informed opinion about what a boomerang is. Dictionaries, and encyclopaedias even more so, abound with definitions of a boomerang in terms of what it is made of or by whom, its supposed use in hunting, and often in fanciful descriptions of its flight which make even the most lurid flying saucer story seem mundane.

For the purposes of this book we shall consider a boomerang primarily in terms of its shape and function: *a basically flat object (with a big bend in the middle) which is capable, if thrown correctly with a spinning motion, of returning to the thrower with a reasonably level trajectory in calm air.*

It is doubtful whether this definition would be greeted with any more acclaim by encyclopaedists or dictionary writers than theirs have been by us, but it is useful in **excluding** from discussion objects which might otherwise be included: non-returning hunting sticks, multi-bladed and saucer-shaped throwing toys, model aeroplanes, and things which have to be thrown into a strong wind or upwards in order to return.

A less elegant way of defining what is meant would be to say that a boomerang is a boomerang-shaped object that boomerangs back to the thrower.

Boomerangs range in wingspan from about 10 centimetres to 1 metre, but the extremes in this range are more in the nature of curiosities than practical boomerangs. The general range in size is from 30 to 60 centimetres in wingspan, with gross weights from 30 to 180 grams. The elbow angle of most boomerangs is within 20 degrees one way or the other of the theoretically ideal angle of 109 degrees. The wings (the 'dingle' arm and the 'lifting' arm) are generally flat on the bottom, except for a bevel cut near one—or in some cases both—of the tips, and they have curved surfaces much the same as aeroplane wings and for the same reason. The curved contours are not symmetrical as is the case with a pair of aeroplane wings; rather, they tend to resemble those of a three-bladed propeller with one of the blades sawn off and thrown away, though they are not quite as highly pitched as the contours of a propeller blade.

A typical boomerang embodying these features is illustrated in **Figure 3.**

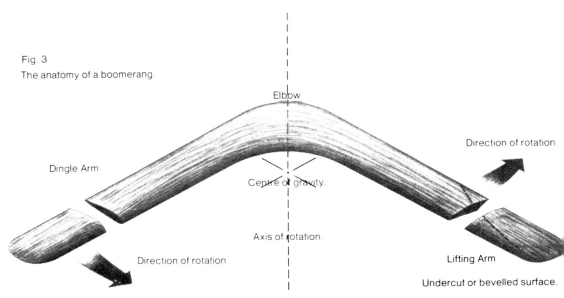

Fig. 3
The anatomy of a boomerang

Elbow

Direction of rotation.

Dingle Arm

Centre of gravity.

Axis of rotation.

Direction of rotation.

Lifting Arm

Undercut or bevelled surface.

An understanding of the principle of boomerang flight is interesting in its own right; it also assists intelligent throwing, and enhances one's appreciation of the beauty and grace of the boomerang in motion. We will therefore consider, in a non-mathematical way, some of the factors that come into play during the returning flight of a boomerang. The subject is not a simple one. It is quite literally true that the orbit of a space satellite round the moon is much easier to explain than the flight of a boomerang on its much smaller orbit round the thrower.

Boomerangs are made to return by forces acting upon them in the air—even though the air in which the boomerang is thrown may be calm, the rapid rotation of the wings creates interesting aerodynamic effects.

Aerodynamics is the study of forces caused by the motion of air, and can be a fairly difficult subject. Fortunately, however, in the case of a boomerang, aerodynamic theory need not be complicated; the effects can be understood simply by thinking of what happens to three types of surfaces in an airstream.

First there is the observation that air causes friction and will slow down an object moving in it. This effect was not really appreciated until the invention of the motor car, the first of which was fairly square in outline with a big blunt radiator in front, a huge flat windscreen a bit farther on, and large flapping mudguards everywhere else. At higher speeds this shape generated a lot

of air friction—something that had not even been thought of with the slower, animal-powered vehicles of previous ages (**Figure 4**).

As we now know, the appropriate remedy for this unwanted air friction (or drag) is to streamline the shape, making it gently rounded or pointed both fore and aft, so that it slips through the air with a minimum of disturbance (**Figure 5**).

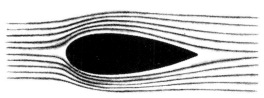

Fig. 5

Second, a flat surface inclined to the airstream as shown in **Figure 6** will experience an upward force, or be lifted. This is the same sort of upthrust that one feels on one's hand when one sticks it out of the window of a moving car or train, catching the breeze at an angle with the palm.

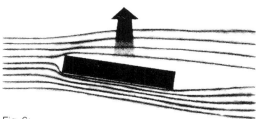

Fig. 6

The third type of interaction between moving air and a solid object is the most difficult of the three to visualise—the lift generated on the upper surface of a curved wing or aerofoil. Birds apply this principle in flying, especially those, such as eagles and seagulls, which specialise in soaring rather than flapping.

This is what happens. The streamlined leading edge of the wing pushes air out of its way both upward and downward as it passes through, slightly compressing the air as this happens. Since the gently bulging

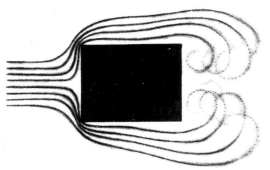

Fig. 4

shape of the top of the wing is different from the essentially flat surface of the bottom, the airflow around it is also different. After the air is compressed and pushed out of the way by the leading edge it climbs over the bulge and then begins to lose its compression as it continues down the sloping top side of the wing **(Figure 7)**.

This is when the most interesting and least appreciated aspect of the aerofoil comes into play.

The tapered upper rear surface of the wing goes all the way down to the flat bottom of the wing. There is therefore an area on the upper rear surface where the air

Fig. 7

pressure is much less than it was before the air was first disturbed. This is tantamount to saying that the wing is sucked up by the region of reduced pressure generated by the wing's forward motion. Additionally, the compression of the air on the underside of the leading edge tends to push up from below. The nett effect is a considerable lift indeed.

The lift very much depends on the fact that the wing shape is not symmetrical: it is flat on the bottom and curved on the top. If it **were** symmetrically tapered on the top and bottom there would be no lift due to airflow.

Referring again to **Figure 3**, it can be seen that these principles of aerodynamic design are incorporated at various places in the construction of a boomerang. First, the leading edges of both arms (wings) are smoothly streamlined to minimise drag. Second, the bevelled or cutaway under-

surface of the lifting arm provides an upthrust when the boomerang rotates in the direction shown. Finally, apart from this bevelled surface the bottom of the boomerang is completely flat, while the top surfaces are contoured to an aerofoil shape which provides lift on rotation.

When a boomerang is thrown by a right-handed thrower it leaves the hand spinning very fast in a counter-clockwise direction. The flat side of a boomerang is to the thrower's right. The plane of the boomerang is almost vertical, being inclined at an angle of almost 60 degrees from the horizontal. The direction of throw is straight ahead, and is neither upward nor downward.

The boomerang travels with a strong forward motion as well as a spinning motion. When a wing is at the top of a rotational cycle its speed through the air therefore equals the speed imparted by the spinning **added to** the forward speed of the boomerang as a whole; conversely, when the same wing is at the bottom of a rotational cycle its speed through the air is less because the speed of rotation is now opposing the forward speed of the boomerang as a whole.[1] Thus, although both wings of a boomerang are contoured to obtain lift from moving air, a wing at the top of its rotational cycle generates more aerodynamic lift (because of its greater speed through the air) than it does at the bottom of the cycle **(Figure 8)**.

Because the boomerang begins its flight in an almost vertical plane, the stronger aerodynamic force at the top of the rotational cycle tries to 'lift' the top of the boomerang into a position even closer to the vertical, thrusting anti-clockwise against the flat under-surface. However, this does not happen, or even begin to happen, because of a characteristic of spinning bodies known as **gyroscopic precession**. This counter-acts the tendency to push the boomerang into a vertical plane by twisting the axis of

[1]
Measurements show the forward speed of a boomerang to be about 95 kilometres per hour, and the tip speed due to rotation to be close to 50 kilometres per hour; at the start of flight the boomerang's top tip therefore moves at about 145 kilometres per hour and the bottom tip at about 45 kilometres per hour.

rotation instead, and the boomerang veers off to the left rather than going straight ahead[2] (see **Figure 10**).

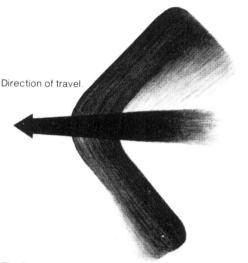

Direction of travel.

Fig. 8

As the boomerang turns to the left it begins to experience another force—an upthrust on its under-surface because it is inclined at an angle to the direction of the airstream. The effect of this is fairly direct: the boomerang begins to rise. As it does so, its forward speed decreases slightly, as does the speed of rotation of the wings, for the energy to raise the boomerang has to come from somewhere.

While all this is going on the original forces which caused the boomerang to veer to the left are still acting, so that the boomerang arcs its way to the left in a sweeping and slightly rising curve. At the top of this curve the blades are spinning noticeably more slowly and the direction of travel has changed remarkably from what it was

originally, being about at right angles to the original direction. In effect, the boomerang is now on its way back to the thrower.

Ideal flight path of a correctly thrown boomerang. The shaded line is the path or 'shadow' of the boomerang seen from above.

Fig. 9

The boomerang, having lost forward air-speed in climbing, no longer experiences up-thrust from the air pushing against its under-surface, so begins to lose altitude. This in turn makes the rotation speed increase, though not sufficiently to create a thrust to-wards the vertical as was the case when the flight began. Instead, the aerodynamic force generated by the rotation is expressed in an extra lift to the wings, so that near the end of the flight the boomerang is rotating in a nearly horizontal plane — floating at a fairly constant height until its forward speed has diminished to zero and its plane of rotation is indeed horizontal. At this point the boom-erang hovers down slowly into the waiting hands of the thrower **(Figure 9)**.

There are other ways of throwing a boomerang which give more varied flight patterns, but they need not be elaborated upon at this stage. In all cases the same basic principles apply.

The flight of a boomerang has been analysed mathematically by several enthu-siasts, mostly notably by G. W. Walker (who was the first) and by Felix Hess, whose work is beyond doubt the most comprehensive; so much so that one is tempted to say that it is virtually the last word, and incapable of fur-ther significant refinement.

2
Gyroscopic precession is a phenomenon that occurs in any spinning object when a twist is applied to its axis of spin or rotation. A child's spinning top, for example, remains virtually motionless when its axis is perfectly upright—but if it leans over slightly, so that the pull of gravity tries to tip it onto its side a gyroscopic force counteracts gravity's pull and instead causes the top to move round in a circle. At first, when the angle of lean is slight, the top moves in a big wide circle; but as it runs out of spin, and leans over more and more the top moves in ever-diminishing circles until it finally succumbs to gravity through friction. The circling caused by a gyroscopic force is known as a **precession**. In the case of a spinning top a circle of several centimetres is observed—with a boomerang, the circle can have a diameter of many metres.

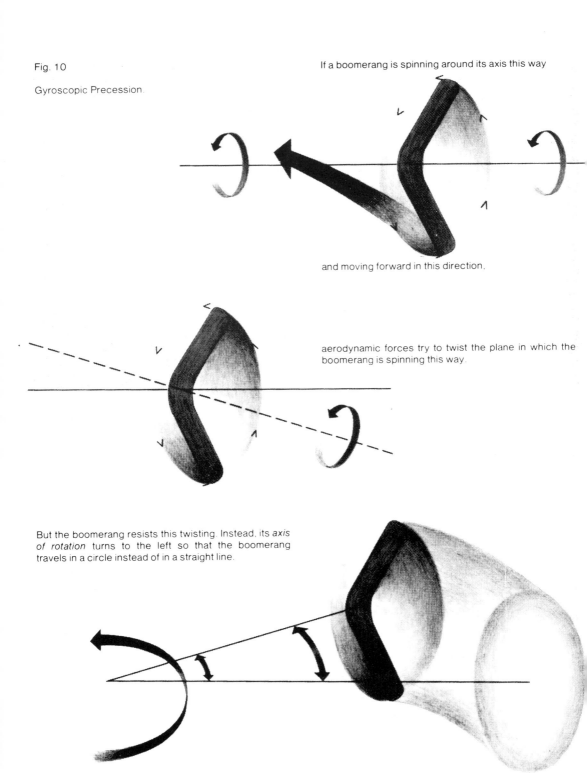

Fig. 10

Gyroscopic Precession.

If a boomerang is spinning around its axis this way

and moving forward in this direction,

aerodynamic forces try to twist the plane in which the boomerang is spinning this way.

But the boomerang resists this twisting. Instead, its *axis of rotation* turns to the left so that the boomerang travels in a circle instead of in a straight line.

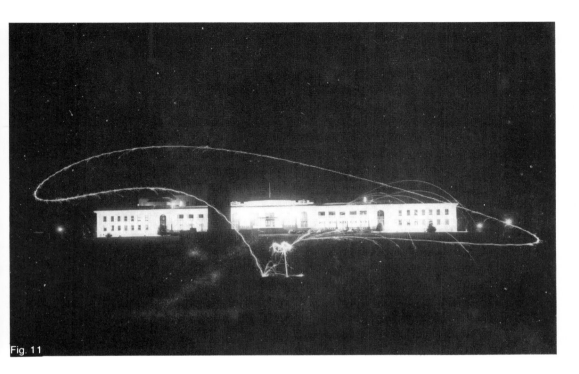

Fig. 11

The beauty of the overall flight may be seen in a time-exposure photograph of a boomerang, taken in the still of the night in front of Parliament House, Canberra. The boomerang had a small 2.5 centimetre section of pyrotechnic sparkler stuck into a hole drilled in the concave side of the boomerang elbow; the sparkler was at the axis of rotation of the boomerang, and thus did not wobble about during the course of the flight **(Figure 11)**.

Having discussed the flight of a boomerang and some of the factors which enter into it, it is of interest to examine how the relative sizes and shapes of boomerangs affect their flight. First, the general outline of a boomerang — why is it bent in the middle?

This concerns the **moment of inertia**[3] of the boomerang. Different geometric shapes have different moments of inertia. The best shape is a thin circular rim, like a bicycle tyre; one of the worst is a straight configuration like a wing spinning about its midpoint. Thus the bent shape of a boomerang is a compromise between these two forms, one of which has a high moment of inertia but no aerodynamic lift, and the other which can have good aerodynamic lift but poor spinning ability.

The lengths of the arms, their thickness, and the wing contours can all be varied so as to produce the sort of flight desired. Long wings rotate relatively slowly and short ones spin fast. Thick wings are capable of more aerodynamic lift, but they also generate more drag in the air and may slow down the spin disastrously (the result is a boomerang which is very lively at first but which runs out of steam after a few seconds). Conversely, thin wings do not lend themselves to fast turnabouts but retain their spin more efficiently.

3
Many people think that **moment of inertia** is that time in the morning when they feel they should get up, but prefer to lie in bed. Technically speaking, this is incorrect. The **moment of inertia** of an object is its inherent ability to keep spinning for a long time. A boomerang obviously requires a high moment of inertia in order to maintain its spin during flight and thus generate aerodynamic lift.

The elbow angle of the boomerang has an important bearing upon the moment of inertia. Within reasonable limits, the more acute (narrow) the elbow angle the higher will be the moment of inertia; conversely, the more obtuse (wide) the angle the lower the moment of inertia for wings that are otherwise the same.

Designing a boomerang is a matter of combining the factors that bring about desirable features for the boomerang one has in mind.

A short range boomerang can be made with a thick section of a low-density wood and a relatively large wingspan. A wind-resistant boomerang can be made with a denser material and short stubby wings that spin very fast but have very little lift.

Long distance boomerangs fall into two types, each with its own set of advantages. The first of these are small, shaped like a question mark without the dot; they have a high moment of inertia because they depart from the traditional shape and approach the concept of a thin rim; their wings have very little camber (or convexity), and they spin very fast indeed.

The second type of long distance boomerang is that pioneered by the late Frank Donnellan. The basic design calls for large, slow-spinning wings set at a widely obtuse angle; as in the previous case, the wings are thin and streamlined. One would expect a low moment of inertia, but this is compensated for by covering the tips and elbow with sheets of lead—thus bringing a good proportion of the mass of the boomerang to the periphery, which produces a higher moment of inertia.

While it is very easy to design a boomerang that performs terribly or falls far short of expectations, there is nevertheless considerable leeway in design and there are probably as many theories about the 'best' aerofoil sections as there are designers.

An interesting (or frustrating, depending on how you look at it) point about boomerangs is that they exist in two forms: right-handed or left-handed, depending on whether they are designed to be thrown by a right-handed or left-handed person.

A left-handed boomerang resembles a right-handed one in the same way as one's left hand resembles the right: they are mirror images of each other. And just about everything that a left-handed boomerang

A left-handed boomerang is the mirror image of a right-handed boomerang.

Fig. 12

does is a mirror image of its right-handed counterpart. It is thrown with the left hand, its plane leans over to the left 30 degrees from the vertical, and it spins in a clockwise direction.

It **is** possible for a right-handed thrower to throw a left-handed boomerang, and vice versa, as will be discussed later, though the type of throw is a bit strained and unnatural. If one tries to throw a left-handed boomerang as one would throw a right-handed model the results are spectacular, if short-lived. Since the aerofoil surfaces of a boomerang operate effectively only when the boomerang is spinning in the correct direction, and since this sort of throw makes them spin in the opposite direction, the boomerang goes out straight, then apparently goes haywire—fluttering wildly to the ground like a one-winged bird.

The boomerang, along with kangaroos and koalas, has become one of the internationally recognised symbols of Australia. It comes as a surprise to many people to realise that while the fauna are unique to Australia, the boomerang is not. Throwing sticks, some of which *do* return and can therefore be classified as true boomerangs, have been found in northern Europe, Egypt, the United States, India and the New Hebrides. The shaded areas indicate the approximate distribution of throwing sticks in prehistoric and historic times.

Modern facsimiles of boomerangs found in the tombs of the Egyptian pharaohs have made satisfactory return flights, and the original 'throwing sticks' can thus be classified as true boomerangs. Others were apparently designed as 'killer sticks' and were probably used in hunting waterfowl and small game. The importance of the throwing sticks may be gauged by their presence in the royal tombs, and the use of gold in their ornamentation.

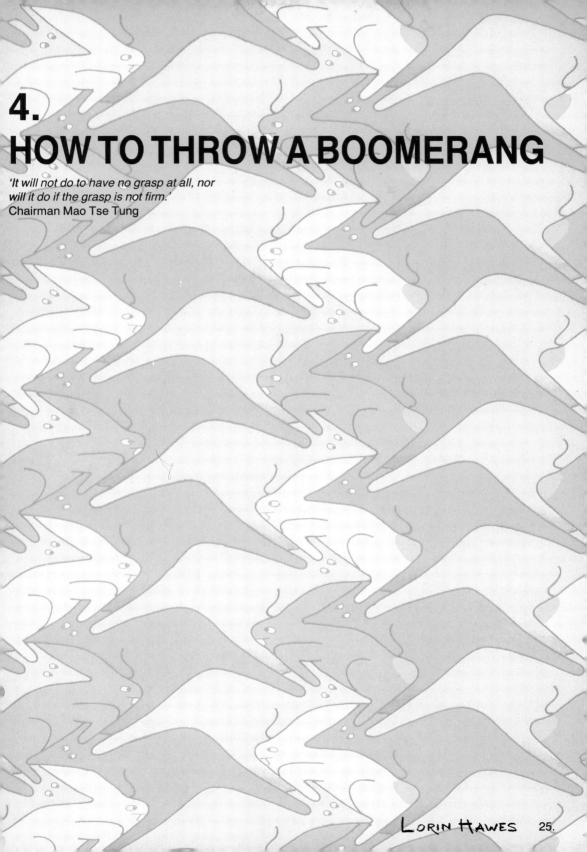

4.
HOW TO THROW A BOOMERANG

'It will not do to have no grasp at all, nor will it do if the grasp is not firm.'
Chairman Mao Tse Tung

LORIN HAWES 25.

Dozens of books have been written about how to hold a golf club, and around the world there are thousands of highly paid professional golfers who teach people which end of a golf club to hold, and how to wrap their fingers around it in various special ways. The art of boomerang throwing has not yet come to such a state—in fact, there is not even a consensus of opinion about which end of the thing to hold! In any case, as long as the boomerang is inclined at the correct angle and thrown with a goodly spin, it should come back regardless of which end has been held.

But what **is** important is the development of techniques that lead to a fast spin in conjunction with an accurate throw. The grasp on a boomerang should be firm, with the index finger hooked round the tip and the flat side of the boomerang pressed against the palm of the hand by the thumb. It is a mistake to hold too much of the boomerang in the hand—about three to four centimetres is ample **(Figure 13)**.

The action of throwing a boomerang is not so much a matter of opening the hand and turning loose the boomerang as it is giving a snappy throw with the hand closed—so that, in leaving, the boomerang has to pull itself free and pivot round the hooked index finger, thus gaining a lot of spin as it does so. If too much of the boomerang is held, the pivoting is more difficult and the spin is reduced.

Fig. 14

The throwing motion of the arm is not unlike the action of cracking a whip. The hand starts its throw at a point behind the shoulder and ends with a snap, straight in front, where it usually stops about an arm's length from the shoulder. Most of the throwing force is transmitted by bending the elbow. There should be no conscious pulling back of the hand before the end of the throw, but rather a smooth follow-through action **(Figure 14)**.

The boomerang is thrown straight ahead—neither upward nor downward. If a breeze is blowing, its direction can be determined by dropping light pieces of grass or leaves, or by noting the drift of smoke from a pipe or cigarette: the boomerang is then aimed about 45 degrees to the right of the direction of the breeze **(Figure 15)**.

Ideally the boomerang should go out reasonably straight at first and then curve to the left[4], climbing slightly until at its farthest point from the thrower, then gliding back in

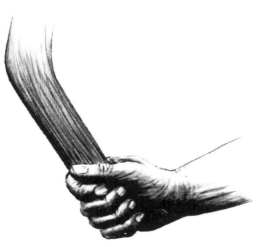

Fig. 13

4
This description applies to a right-handed boomerang. If a left-handed model is being thrown it should be aimed 45 degrees to the **left** of the direction of the breeze. The boomerang will curve to the **right**, and its overall trajectory will be clockwise.

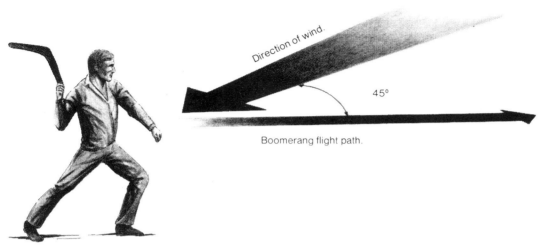

Direction of wind.

45°

Boomerang flight path.

Fig. 15
Compensating for wind.

an arc that brings it over the head of the thrower, where it hovers slowly down. Unfortunately several factors prevent this idealised flight—especially for the beginner.

The most common error in throwing a boomerang is not finding the correct angle of incline. Most people **know** that the boomerang should be horizontal when it leaves the hand, and that words (such as these) which suggest otherwise are nonsense. Hence, when they have a boomerang in their hand for the first time, they lean it over at a flat angle—and then watch it go soaring straight up into the sky. All too often the common reaction is 'I guess I didn't throw it hard enough' and another attempt using the same incorrect technique with more brute force. The result: a boomerang rendered into matchwood, its life brought to a premature end without its ever having performed in the manner for which it was intended.

Caution No. 1: The boomerang should be inclined at an angle of about 60 degrees from the horizontal and thrown straight ahead—but gently at first. If it goes too high.

the angle should be adjusted closer to the vertical. If it does not go high enough, and lands prematurely, the angle should be flattened so that the boomerang leans over more towards the horizontal plane **(Figure 16)**.

Perhaps the second most frequent error is not adjusting correctly for the effect of the wind. If the wind is blowing any more than five kilometres an hour, don't even try throwing a boomerang at all—put the thing away and fly a kite until the wind drops. Any breeze at all, no matter how slight, will affect the boomerang in two ways: it will deflect the boomerang to the right or to the left, and will also tend to blow it back behind the point where it would otherwise land.

The solutions are simple. Every throw, if properly interpreted, tells the thrower what correction should be applied to the next: if the boomerang lands to the right of the thrower it should be aimed more to the left; conversely, if it lands to the left it should be aimed more to the right (see **Figure 17);** if it has gone too high and landed behind the thrower then the angle of lean should be closer to the vertical.

Fig. 16
Correct and incorrect flight paths as seen from the side.

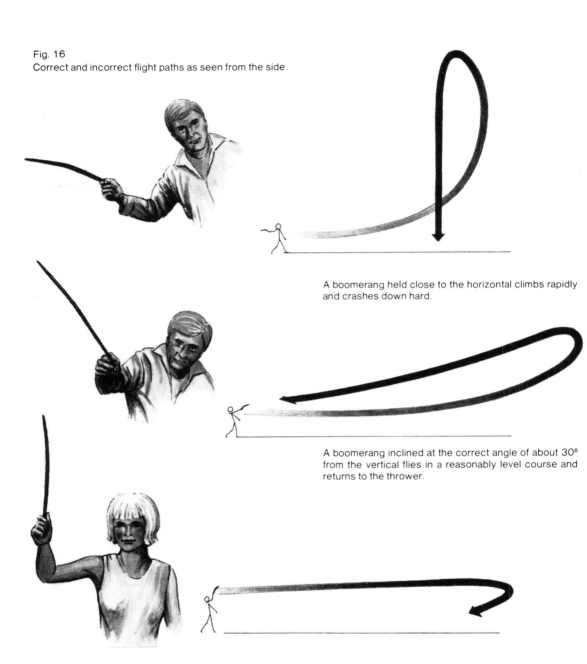

A boomerang held close to the horizontal climbs rapidly and crashes down hard.

A boomerang inclined at the correct angle of about 30° from the vertical flies in a reasonably level course and returns to the thrower.

A boomerang held close to the vertical does not gain sufficient elevation and crashes into the ground.

Fig. 17

Flight paths in windy conditions, as seen from above.

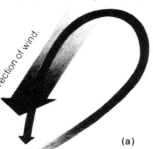

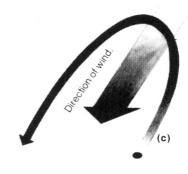

(a)

(b)

(c)

(a) Thrown approximately 45° to the right of the wind's direction, the boomerang should return.

(b) Thrown too far to the right of the wind, the boomerang will land to the right.

(c) Thrown too close to or to the left of the wind, the boomerang will land to the left.

Caution No. 2: Always allow for any breeze, no matter how slight, bearing in mind that it is stronger five metres up than it is at ground level.

Although it does not really matter which end of the boomerang is held, there **are**-differences, however, in the throwing characteristics. In practical terms, while these differences may be slight, they can be used to good advantage and may even mean the difference between failure and success, depending upon the thrower and the boomerang.

The Lifting Arm Throw

Perhaps the most obvious way to hold a boomerang is to grasp it like a sickle, at the lifting arm end. A big advantage is that the boomerang pivots round the index finger to the maximum extent (especially if the boomerang is 'cocked' back toward the elbow of the arm before throwing) and hence acquires a very fast spin. This throwing technique is followed, almost to the exclusion of all others, by Aborigines and by many other throwers as well. A serious disadvantage is that this type of throw is rather unwieldy, and there is a tendency for the boomerang to lean over a little too far and hence go high.

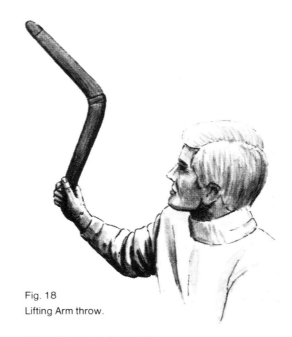

Fig. 18

Lifting Arm throw.

The Dingle Arm Throw

When a boomerang spins in the air it balances itself round its centre of gravity—a point usually located about two or three centimetres away from the inside of the boomerang's elbow. A boomerang held and thrown by the dingle arm therefore has this weight behind the hand; as the boomerang is thrown the weight automatically follows the hand in the same way as a rock tied to a string. This is, inherently, a more accurate type of throw than the lifting arm method, where the centre of gravity of the boomerang is pushed from behind by the hand and thus has a tendency to veer off to the left or right.

The dingle arm throw generally imparts less spin to the boomerang but gives a stronger forward motion resulting in a slightly longer range. There is less tendency for a boomerang to go high when thrown by the dingle arm, and this must be allowed for when changing from one type of throw to the other; with the lifting arm throw the boomerang is held slightly closer to the vertical angle.

Among the Aborigines, who have deeply rooted father-to-son traditions about how to throw a boomerang, the dingle arm throw is virtually unknown. Presumably the early Aborigines used the lifting arm throw and this has been perpetuated through successive generations.

Fig. 19
Dingle Arm throw.

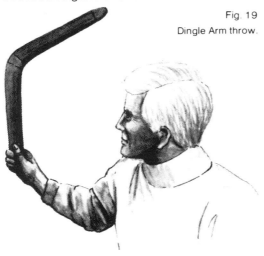

The Elbow Throw

An unusual way to throw a boomerang is to hold it at the elbow, pinching it tightly between the thumb and first knuckle of the index finger. This throw is by far the most difficult to master, is virtually impossible with large boomerangs, and is not as accurate as either the lifting arm or the dingle arm throws. Why bother with it? The answer is that the true boomerang enthusiast wants to be proficient in all aspects of boomerang throwing. This technique also emphasises the point that it does not really matter how one throws the thing so long as the angle of lean and the spin are correctly applied.

In making the throw a great deal of wrist action is necessary. To obtain the firmest possible grip, any wax coating should be removed from the elbow. Perhaps because this throw is the most difficult—and, to the layman, the 'impossible'—it gives the thrower the greatest degree of satisfaction when executed to perfection.

Elbow throw.
Fig. 20

One final point. It is possible to throw a boomerang too hard. There is a definite tendency among beginners to assume that if a boomerang has not gone properly it should be thrown much harder next time. In fact, only a moderate throw is required for a perfect flight. The wise thrower conserves strength so as to be able to keep throwing all day rather than be forced to give up, after only a few hours, by a handful of blisters or a dislocated shoulder.

There is no real harm in throwing a boomerang very strongly if it is done properly; for some effects, such as making it go round twice, it may be necessary. Normally, however, one should regard boomerang throwing as being akin to watch repairing, in that skill is much more important than brute force in achieving success.

5.
BOOMERANG SAFETY

'I shall turn my back on this.'
Richard M. Nixon

LORIN HAWES 31.

Safety is a point that comes to the minds of most people as soon as boomerangs are mentioned, probably because of the myth that boomerangs are designed to kill a kangaroo and then return to the hunter—who sticks the boomerang under his belt, grabs the kangaroo by the tail and drags it off into the sunset. The truth is less dramatic. Boomerang throwing could be classed on about the same danger level as model aeroplane flying, and it is certainly not as dangerous as so-called 'safe' sports like softball or cricket.

There is of course an ever-present chance that the boomerang is going to hit somebody, some time. But that is hardly surprising, since boomerang throwing is the only sport in the world in which the thrower is also the target.

It is therefore important to make sure that, even if someone gets hit with a boomerang,

there are no injuries. Fortunately this is a fairly simple matter. Although the tips of the boomerang may be spinning rather fast, the speed of the boomerang through the air is relatively slow. Normally, all one has to do to avoid injury is to keep an eye on the boomerang and turn one's back to it if in danger of being hit. It isn't that turning one's back will cause the boomerang to veer off course—but a boomerang can cause injury only if it hits someone in the eye, face, or wherever there is a bone very close to the skin.

Spectators invariably gather where boomerangs are being thrown. It is vital to warn them, too, to turn their backs—otherwise they might try to run out of the way but (because of the peculiar trajectory of the boomerang) run into the boomerang instead. In addition to this warning, it is a good idea (if possible) to keep the spectators upwind of

the throwing area, and considerably farther away than the maximum range of the boomerang. Always check before each throw to make sure that some little child isn't toddling onto the field where it can get hit.

While safety considerations affecting possible injuries to people are of obvious importance, two other points should be well to the fore in the thoughts of the boomerang thrower: damage to property, and damage to the boomerang itself.

A list of all property damaged by boomerangs since their invention would in reality be rather small. Broken windows come to mind immediately, but in practice there is no justification for this. While it is unlikely that the owner of a greenhouse would welcome the establishment of a boomerang club next door, it is seldom (if ever) that one hears of a window being broken by a boomerang.

Obviously one **could** break a window at close quarters by deliberately throwing at it a boomerang or any other hard object. But, normally, when a boomerang hits a window it is a glancing blow and quite harmless.

It is more likely that a boomerang will hit a car parked near a throwing field. While it is again unlikely that any real damage will be inflicted, in the eyes of the car owner any little scratch is important, and unkind words may be directed towards the boomerang thrower in the subsequent argument about whether or not the thrower should get the boomerang back.

The most likely mishap is damage to the boomerang itself. Undeniably, this is a real tragedy for the owner. This can happen if the boomerang crashes down hard once too often, hits something hard and unyielding in flight, or hits a rock on landing. Preventive measures are self-evident. One should not throw a boomerang incorrectly or lend it to others who might; nor should one throw it in rocky terrain, in places where there are too many trees, or in cemeteries with tall tombstones and statues everywhere.

A final word to those who disregard the advice in this chapter and end up holding two pieces of boomerang in their hands: some of the new five-minute epoxy glues are ideal for mending even the most serious breaks in a boomerang, and no thrower should be without the stuff. A boomerang can be back in the air ten minutes after being broken, and if the repair is carefully carried out the flight will be the same as before.

SAVE TREES FOR BOOMERANGS!

6.
ADVANCED TECHNIQUES...
AND PROBLEMS

*'The various modes of enjoyment are not
for all times or for all persons, but they
should only be used at the proper time...'*
The Kama Sutra

LORIN HAWES 35.

Once the thrower has experienced for the first time the thrill of hurling a boomerang outward into orbit, and of seeing it return precisely to the starting point, he knows that he has truly tasted one of life's sublime experiences and will want to do it again and again. Unfortunately this is not always possible: fate seems, at times, to make the boomerang go completely haywire, and this is accentuated whenever there are spectators.

Practice is, of course, the best cure. If one remembers what one did on each good throw and tries to repeat it, the throws will become better and better. There is a corresponding elevation of one's throwing standards as this goes on: whereas at first the thrower is delighted when a throw comes 80 per cent back, after a while he will curse bitterly if he has to move even one foot from the starting point in order to make a one-handed catch. This chapter will help expedite this state of affairs by condensing the knowledge gained by the authors, after many hundreds of thousands of throws, into a set of useful working principles.

Let us begin by modifying some of the points made in the chapter 'How to Throw a Boomerang' (not that any of the material in it is incorrect!). There, the factors affecting a throw and a flight were treated, for the sake of clarity, as though they were independent of one another. Of course, they are not. The factors of spin, angle of lean, strength of throw, direction and elevation of aim, are all interrelated. Except in rare cases this interrelationship will be different for each throw of a given boomerang, and can never be the same for any two boomerangs.

While the particular combination of factors set out earlier (throwing straight out, leaning the boomerang at 60 degrees from the horizontal, aiming 45 degrees to the right of the wind's direction) is valid as a starting point, experimentation shows that certain changes can be made which will still bring the boomerang back nicely. This adds variety to the throws and stops them from being identical (though beginners achieve variety without really trying!).

Interestingly enough there is an effortless technique, acquired almost universally by professional throwers and by well-practised amateurs, which seems to contradict just about all of the previous instructions. The boomerang is aimed low, held almost completely flat, and thrown very gently—but with terrific spin. And it works well. It also causes some embarrassment when the expert thrower advises the beginner to throw in one way and then goes out himself and does the very opposite! The key to success in this type of throw is the ability to impart to the boomerang a very fast spin which compensates for leaning the thing over at an angle that would normally be considered too flat.

It all boils down to the fact that any one feature of a flight is usually governed by more than one factor—for example, the height to which a boomerang goes. Obviously if one aims it high it will go high. However, it will also go high if one leans it over at too flat an angle and then aims it straight out.

Another example concerns whether the boomerang lands to the right or to the left. The primary control is any breeze that is blowing, and a consequent alteration of the direction of the throw. The secondary control of direction is a more subtle combination of the angle of lean, force of throw, and how high one aims.

Good illustrations of the intelligent application of these secondary controls are found in two throwing conditions encountered frequently—throwing when it is windy, and throwing when it is absolutely dead calm.

Throwing in windy conditions

Wind is the biggest source of frustration for the keen boomeranger. Few areas of human activity (with the possible exception of the long distance smoke-ring blowing) are so affected by wind as is boomerang throwing. Not only is the boomerang in the air for a long time, but it is subjected to breezes in a way different from other airborne objects. An arrow, for example, is deflected to the right or to the left by a crosswind, and is speeded up or slowed down by a tailwind or headwind. All one has to do to correct for the wind is to aim a bit to the right or left, or up or down from where one normally would, then pull back on the string, close one's eyes, and let fly. The arrow automatically goes to the centre of the target.

But because a boomerang makes a complete circle, the wind is at some stage blowing from the right or from the left; it is a headwind for part of the flight and a tailwind for part; and, in addition to affecting the destination through the overall movement of the air mass relative to the boomerang, the wind and its eddies can tip the axis of rotation of the boomerang, and can generate powerful upthrust forces on the underside which send the thing sky high where it catches even more wind. These points, to put it mildly, do not contribute to the ease of making an accurate throw.

There are two basically different methods of throwing when it is windy, depending upon whether one wants to eliminate the upthrust forces by presenting (a) a minimum aerofoil to the wind, or (b) a perpendicular surface to the wind that tends to be blown back rather than up. In the first of these methods the boomerang is thrown very gently with a minimum of spin, holding it quite flat. Essentially, the wind blows it back.

Fig. 21

When throwing in extreme wind, the boomerang should be leaned over to the left so that it is partially upside down, and should be aimed upward rather than straight ahead.

The second method, more satisfying to the connoisseur, is to hold the boomerang beyond the vertical so that it leans inward instead of outward. The boomerang is aimed slightly up into the sky rather than being thrown straight ahead as usual. Thus it rises as soon as it leaves the hand, but because it is leaned over the 'wrong way', it opposes the rise and is flying about level when it has turned through a quarter to a third of the circle **(Figure 21)**.

Fig. 22

Flight path for extreme wind correction.

Most importantly, the accompanying gyroscopic precession has by this time altered the angle of lean so that it is vertical—thus the boomerang does not experience any upward or downward forces at the moment when it is exposed most strongly to the full blast of the wind. After this point the boomerang swoops down fairly low behind and to the left of the thrower, then rises and hovers to the right of the thrower before chopping its way back against the wind for a perfect return **(Figure 22)**.

Bear in mind that in windy conditions the spectacular and often disastrous uplift of the boomerang occurs on the return part of the orbit: on the way out the tendency of the wind is to blow a normally thrown boomerang **down** and into the ground. Rapidly changing winds are difficult to counteract, as are momentary whirlwinds. An anti-clockwise whirlwind has the effect of killing the returning action since it reduces the airspeed of the boomerang; a clockwise whirlwind has the effect of causing a faster than usual turnaround, and an increase in the spin.

Throwing when it is completely calm

Normally there is a gentle breeze, and it is seldom that the air is really dead-calm. Many throwers get into the habit of relying upon this seemingly ever-present breeze to 'give direction' to their throw. This presents a quandary when the breeze does stop completely—for instead of coming back to the thrower the boomerang may fall short, typically landing in front of the thrower and to the left. Aiming higher does not help at all; under these conditions it makes the boomerang go into an oddly S-shaped curve, veering away to the left after approaching in front of the thrower.

The best technique when throwing in dead-calm conditions is to aim low, applying a lot of spin. The boomerang should just miss the ground on the outward journey, go up high and almost stall, then swoop back down again, miss the ground and rise to a good hover by the thrower. Calm conditions are an exacting test not only of the skill of the thrower but also of the accuracy of the design and construction of the boomerang.

Catching a boomerang

To the uninformed, the act of catching a boomerang in mid-air with bare hands is akin to the famous stage act of catching a bullet in the teeth, or walking on hot coals, or the like—a result, no doubt, of the primeval myth that the boomerang's function is to kill kangaroos. In fact it is much easier to catch a properly thrown boomerang than a cricket ball or baseball. No ball slows to a stop in mid-air and hovers waiting to be caught. But a boomerang does, and all one has to do is to clasp it flat between the hands **(Figure 23)**.

Catching it with one hand is a little more difficult. The technique is to grab — preferably with the left hand[5] — at the centre of the boomerang when it is coming in from the left in a slow hover after throwing so that the boomerang comes in slightly high and over the left shoulder. If the thumb is pointed straight down and the four fingers are held tightly together the boomerang will slip in automatically **(Figure 24)**.

Catching a boomerang is a mark of some skill. It separates the sheep from the goats, as it were, for it embodies the high degree of skill and accuracy required to bring the boomerang in close enough to be caught, the knowledge of where to be when the boomerang begins its hover, and a touch of co-ordination to finalise. It is something which pleases spectators enormously. Raw beginners unfamiliar with the flight paths of boomerangs should not attempt it, and it is strongly recommended when learning the art that a glove be worn on the catching hand to cushion the shock and cutting action should the catch be wrongly made.

5
This way, if a finger is injured, throwing can continue with the right hand in a normal way. Left-handers, conversely, should use their right hand for a one-handed catch; the boomerang should come in over their right shoulder.

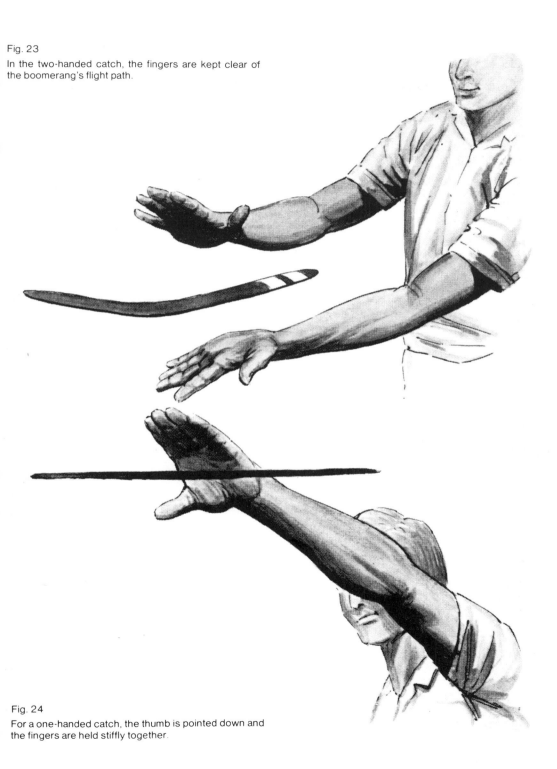

Fig. 23
In the two-handed catch, the fingers are kept clear of the boomerang's flight path.

Fig. 24
For a one-handed catch, the thumb is pointed down and the fingers are held stiffly together.

Occasionally a finger joint or nail may be bruised or broken through misjudgement, but this need not be a deterrent: most conjurers' supply shops stock what is known as a thumb tip, which slips over an injured finger, protects it from further knocks and allows it to heal normally while still in use — catching boomerangs!

Throwing a left-handed boomerang

It's awkward, but a right-handed thrower **can** throw a left-handed boomerang (and vice versa) through some interesting contortion that ends up with the boomerang leaning over at the same angle to the left, and spinning in the same direction, as it would do if thrown by a left-hander.

The right-handed thrower grasps the left-handed boomerang in the right hand with the flat side inward and down, throwing it in a sweep across the face that begins above the right shoulder in a manner reminiscent of a tennis smash. Wind corrections are of course reversed, since a left-handed boomerang must be thrown about 45 degrees to the left of any breeze, but otherwise the general principles applying to right-handed boomerangs work the same way for left-handed ones. Catching a left-handed boomerang is a challenge and a test of the thrower's intelligence, for the interesting and familiar gyrations during the hover are reversed, so that the boomerang appears to veer off in exactly the opposite way to which the thrower is accustomed.

By similar techniques a left-hander can throw a right-handed boomerang.

Throwing two together

A real test of the thrower's skill is to throw two boomerangs together and catch them both on the return. To do this, use two boomerangs which are virtually identical; alter one by sanding a flat surface on the top of its dingle arm, and increase the overall lift of the other boomerang so that its range is reduced slightly (this keeps the two from colliding in mid-air. In throwing, the flat side of the shorter-range boomerang is pressed against the flat spot on the upper surface of the other so that the two boomerangs are parallel. They are then thrown in the normal way, but a little harder since one is contending with twice the usual weight. They should stay within a few feet of each other throughout the flight, landing together unless the thower is able to catch them first.

Turbulence

As we know or vaguely suspect, one of the chief strategies in sailboat racing is to get one's boat in such a position that it has good access to "clean" air — fresh and undisturbed, while ensuring that the other boats are in a "wind shadow", that is, they receive the breeze only after the wind stream has been affected by the first boat.

Many think the reason for this is that the velocity of the air has been reduced by the leading boat, but actually this effect is rather small. The real reason is that the air has become turbulent after being affected by the first boat. It no longer flows in a uniform direction but contains eddies and cross currents which rob it of its power, even several hundred feet away.

Roughly the same thing can happen when boomerangs are thrown into a breeze disturbed by swirling around buildings and other solid obstructions, and through the branches and leaves of trees.

Trees are especially bad in this regard, for the feel of the air on the throwers face does not reveal the turbulence within. To all intents and purposes the throwing conditions may seem to be ideal... until a boomerang is thrown. It acts all right on the outward journey but acts "dead" on the return, falls short and does not hover at all well. Except for giving as much spin as possible and otherwise throwing gently, there isn't a great deal that can be done to overcome the reduced lifting power of turbulent air.

Thin Air

Throwing boomerangs at high altitudes is an interesting change from throwing at sea level. The boomerangs have a greatly extended range as mentioned later on, but the thinness of the air makes it necessary to apply as much spin as possible to get anything like a reasonable return from a sea level boomerang. Much more care is required in throwing to attain any degree of accuracy at all, and the graceful hovering effects seen at lower altitudes just don't happen. Catching becomes a risky business as the boomerangs come in at speed.

These difficulties are of course due to the fact that the air is less and the aerodynamic lift is reduced — while the force of gravity remains about the same.

Twist and Warp

Be they made of wood, metal or plastic, boomerangs can become distorted from their ideal shape (usually flat). Plastic and metal can become distorted on impact or by being bent during storage. Wood has the additional disadvantage of sometimes shrinking unevenly when it loses moisture, and to a lesser extent, of swelling unevenly when regaining it. (**Warpage** refers to a simple bending of the plane of the boomerang: **twisting** to a compound or helical distortion.)

Probably the easiest way to check a boomerang for distortions of these types is to use a large mirror* and two small pieces of flat plywood about an inch or 3cm. square, and which have the same thickness. Scraps from boomerang construction do very nicely.

The basic idea in the procedure is that the "flat" or underside of the middle of the elbow

of the boomerang is pressed firmly against one of the plywood pieces — which in turn is pressed against the mirror — as shown in figure 43.

If the boomerang is perfectly flat then the second piece of plywood should pass exactly between the mirror and the boomerang; if the "flat" or underside of the boomerang is actually not flat at all but concave then the second piece of plywood will not pass at all. And if it is convex then it will pass with space to spare. The amount and nature of the distortion is thus directly observable.

Flight paths of different boomerangs will react differently to distortion, but for medium range boomerangs of the traditional Aboriginal shape as constructed in Chapter 8 it is best to have the boomerang either quite flat or else to have a bit of "convexity" of the flat side so that the tips are raised from the flat plane by an amount between 1% to 2% of the wingspan.

Plastic and metal boomerangs are fairly straightforward to adjust. In the case of the former, judicious force can be supplemented by heat to make the job easier and the results more permanent.

Wooden boomerangs have the problem that if the distortion is severe it may take a while to get them flat again. Wrapping in a damp cloth and careful clamping in a position of reversed warp or twist should affect a cure within a week. The distortion in a wooden boomerang probably developed over a long time and it is not reasonable to expect to cure it instantly: the price of impatience could well be a boomerang strained past its limit of coherence — that is, you end up with two pieces of it in your hands.

---

* This is usually the most readily obtainable large flat surface.

Early Boomerangs
From the Museum of Western Australia, Perth.

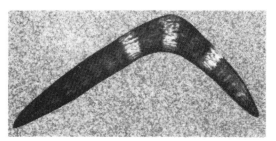

9 Collected in Beagle Bay, 1900.
Weight: 285 grams.

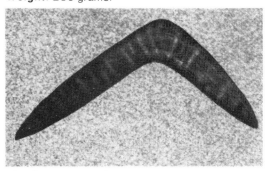

10 Collected in Cygnet Bay, 1910. Made of iron!
Weight: 285 grams.

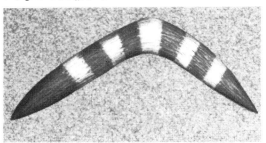

11 Collected in West Kimberley region, 1912.
Weight: 136 grams.

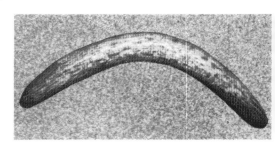

12 North-western WA, 1912.
Weight: 150 grams.

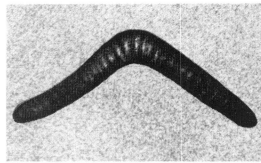

13 Murchison, WA.
Weight: 300 grams.

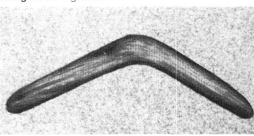

14 This (unknown locality) boomerang is very badly weathered but looks the most promising regarding flight; the dingle arm is very thin and all bevelled surfaces appear quite reasonable.

KEY TO COMPARATIVE SIZES

30.5 cm

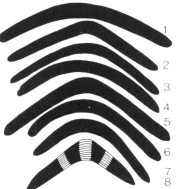

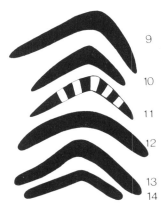

7.
RECORDS AND PERFORMANCES

'I am the greatest!'
Muhammad Ali

Every four years the suggestion is put forth in the Australian press that boomerang throwing should become an Olympic Sport. It is argued that this would increase national prestige and 'put Australia on the map' — while at the same time increasing the nation's tally of Olympic gold medals, tacitly presuming a centuries-old advantage in technique.

It is highly unlikely that this will ever come to be. Boomerang throwing always has been, and is likely to remain, an individual type of sport, and one which defies either competitive measurement or being incorporated into some sort of game. There are many minor reasons for this: the difficulty in defining a satisfactory flight path so as to exclude missiles which merely glide up and back at the steep angle; the varying views about whether the goal should be the attainment of high accuracy of return, or, the ability to throw the boomerang the greatest distance (or the shortest distance), or, again, the performance of some other mind-boggling feat.

On top of these small but basic difficulties is the problem of classifying, standardising and perhaps handicapping boomerangs in some systematic way so as to be fair to all competitors, as in a yacht race.

But the one problem which makes all others pale into insignificance is wind—its effect, from any fair competitive standpoint, is utterly disastrous. This bears examination in greater detail.

First, as has been previously discussed, wind has a tremendous effect upon accurate boomerang flight. A light breeze can be beneficial in some cases but a slightly stronger one can be a calamity. Unfortunately the dividing line between these two conditions is commonly exceeded on a normal day. The sad fact is that it is usually too windy to throw at all.[6]

In the case of long distance throwing a stiff breeze is a distinct advantage — especially if a fairly heavy, aerodynamically neutral boomerang is used. Although it

would not be capable of returning on a calm day, if it is thrown in the lee of a large building or row of trees so that it goes out a long way before catching the wind, it will be lofted upward and then blown back. To the purist, this verges on cheating — and it is rather sad that virtually all existing long distance records have been set in circumstances similar to this. If records are to have any meaning at all, they must be set under windless conditions.

Second, any competition or exhibition must be equally fair to all competitors and interesting to spectators as well. In any typical outdoor situation subject to air currents the first of these conditions is never achieved. The wind comes and goes capriciously and, with it, the throwers' chances. If a competitor refuses to throw until the wind drops (or rises, if he is counting on it for help!) then he ruins the enjoyment for the spectators and the affair becomes as dull as a bad cricket match. There are no happy solutions other than moving into a very large building like the Sydney Opera House for competitions.

Long distance competitions pose their own problems, for in addition to all of the preceding difficulties there is the problem of determining accurately just how far from the thrower the boomerang really goes. For athletic events like javelin throwing or long jumping this is easy: one merely measures, with a tape, the distance from the throwing or take-off point to the landing point. But how does one measure the spot on the ground that was directly underneath a boomerang at its farthest point from the thrower?

Altitude has a marked effect on the range of a boomerang. The fact that all long distance 'records' have been set at or near sea level suggests that if one wants to break all such records and make a big name, one could do so by raising the level of one's throwing — in a literal as well as a figurative sense. A boomerang with a range at sea level of 12 metres will travel outward about 18 metres at a height of 1,800 metres

6
This point is not always emphasised by people who make a living selling boomerangs.

(Denver) or 35 metres at a height of 3,800 metres (Lake Titicaca). This poses an interesting problem unless the world centre of boomerang expertise is to move from Australia to the slopes of Mt Everest.

Despite these difficulties (or perhaps because they are oblivious to them) boomerang throwers all over the world hold competitions, argue over old records and set new ones, and in so doing make fascinating throws which act as an inspiration and challenge to others.

The following records include some that may or may not have been set with wind assistance or hindrance, some that may have been set under the pressure of open competition under less than ideal conditions, and some that may have been subject to errors in measurement. Nevertheless, it is interesting to examine achievements indicating the kinds of throws that have been made in the recent past. For the most part they have been compiled by Ben Ruhe of the Smithsonian Institution, World Registrar and Co-ordinator of Boomerang Activities, who prefaces them with these words: 'Anyway, records shouldn't be taken too seriously. Sport for its own sake is the thing. If the standards cited are taken as an indication of the possibilities for fun in the contemporary sport of boomeranging then the following compilation will have served a useful purpose.'

Greatest distance thrown: 146.3 metres (Frank Donnellan, Centennial Park, Sydney, Australia. May 4, 1934.)

Greatest distance thrown under windless conditions: 47.5 metres (Lorin Hawes, Mudgeeraba, Australia.)

Most consecutive one-handed catches: 36 (Dennis Maxwell, Dinley, Australia.)

Accuracy: 11 straight catches without moving either foot (Robert Boys, Merriam, Kansas, USA.)

Shortest range: 1.85 metres (Bevan Rayner, Sydney, Australia, using a 40 centimetre boomerang.)

Most consecutive catches: 129 (John McMahon, South Padre Island, Texas, USA.)

Triple throwing: Three boomerangs thrown and collected in 18 seconds (Willi Urban, Leutershausen, Germany.)

Shortest time for 10 catches of a boomerang: 2 minutes 9 seconds (Lorin Hawes, Mudgeeraba, Australia, at 1973 Australian National Championships in Canberra.)

Smallest boomerang to go 25 yards (22.9 metres): 11.12 centimetres (made and thrown by the Burwell brothers, Slacks Creek, Queensland, Australia.)

Largest boomerang to go 25 yards (22.9 metres): 78.7 centimetres (made and thrown by Roy Johns, Griffith, NSW, at the 1971 Australian National Championships.)

Best throw under worst conditions: 98 metres in a wind of 32 kilometres per hour (H.A. Smith, Sussex, England.)

Best throw around a structure: Felix Hess of Groningen, Holland, threw a boomerang completely around the Washington Monument, which has a base measuring 16.9 metres by 16.9 metres.

Best feat with feet: Joe Timbrey of La Perouse, Australia, has on many occasions, one of which was in the presence of Queen Elizabeth II, thrown a boomerang and caught it with his bare feet on the return.

Most courageous throw: The late Frank Donnellan of Parramatta, NSW, would throw a boomerang while blind-folded, standing motionless and allowing the boomerang to hit an apple on his head.

Best double throw: Howard Baker, Balby, England, once threw a right-handed and a left-handed boomerang together for a landing one on top of the other between his feet.

NOTE: These records were current in 1975; compare with Chapter 9!

. . . and so it goes. The possibilities are almost endless with this versatile instrument. The height of frustration in these endeavours is when a thrower has made a stupendous perfect throw of this nature and then finds that nobody was watching at the time.

So many enthusiasts in Australia claim the title of 'World Champion Boomerang Thrower' that it is something of a novelty to encounter a good thrower who does not claim this title. While it is unlikely that a regular and truly international series of competitions could ever be organised or held to give credence to any such title, there are at present two widely followed codes for competitive throwing which serve as a step in the right direction—those of the Boomerang Association of Australia, and those of the Mudgeeraba Creek Emu Racing and Boomerang Throwing Association.

B.A.A. rules, followed in Victoria, southern New South Wales and the Australian Capital Territory, offer a means for assessing throws on a points system that recognises the skills involved in accuracy, range, and catching.

Under these rules a throwing field is marked out in concentric circles spaced four, eight and 12 metres from the throwing point. To qualify for scoring, a boomerang must go outward at least 20 metres. Six points are awarded if it returns within the four-metre circle, four points if within the eight-metre circle, and two points if within the 12-metre circle. If the boomerang is caught anywhere on its return four additional points are awarded. Extra points are awarded for longer distance throws provided that they return within the 12-metre circle: two points if the range exceeds 30 metres and four points if it exceeds 40 metres. After each contestant has had an agreed number of throws the points are tabulated and the winner declared.

The M.C.E.R.B.T.A. rules, followed in Queensland, Western Australia, Southern Rhodesia and Washington, DC, separate the sport into several categories, with separate simple competitions for each. Because of their versatility and wide acceptance, these rules are reprinted in full:

Mudgeeraba Creek Emu Racing and Boomerang Throwing Association
Mudgeeraba, Queensland

Rules of Boomerang Competition, as amended to 1965. The competition is divided into five sections representing the five major divisions of boomerang skill. Suitable prizes will be awarded to the winner of each section, and a grand prize to the contestant amassing the greatest overall number of points from the various sections. Specific rules for these sectional contests are as follows:

1 Distance: *Boomerang to be thrown the greatest distance—a judge to position himself under the flight path of the boomerang at its point of greatest distance from the thrower, and the judge shall determine the position on the ground corresponding to the position of maximum extension. The distance of the throw is to be measured accurately from this point to the original throwing position with a calibrated tape, and corrected for inaccuracy by subtracting the distance away from the original throwing position that the boomerang lands, regardless of the direction of the correction. Thus, if a boomerang goes 60 metres away from the thrower, and lands or is caught three metres away from the throwing point, a distance of 57 metres would be recorded.*

2   Accuracy: *Boomerang to be thrown around a telegraph or similar pole at least 13.7 metres (15 yards) away. The number of steps that the thrower has to go from the point of throwing to the point of retrieving or catching are counted for three successive throws, the winner being the thrower whose number of paces is least.*

3   Catching: *All contestants throw simultaneously and attempt to catch their boomerangs in their bare hands without dropping them. The thrower with the largest number of consecutive catches is the winner. Contestants are eliminated on dropping or failing to catch the boomerang. Boomerangs must go outward at least 5.5 metres (six yards) from the thrower.*

4   Short Distance: *Contestants begin at a preselected distance from a large flat wall or wire netting screen, each throwing his boomerang until all have done so. Throwers whose boomerangs touch the obstacle are disqualified, and the remainder advance one metre closer to the obstacle and repeat. This is continued until no more than five throwers remain, at which point the rate of advance is reduced to 30 centimetres (one foot).*

5   Continuous Throwing: *Two boomerangs to be used. The object is to maintain at least one boomerang in the air at a time, and the contestant who achieves this for the greatest number of throws is the winner.*

Points: *In each section, five points are awarded to the winner, three to the runner-up, two to third place, and one to fourth place. In the event of ties, the contest shall be re-run for the tied competitors only, to determine placings. In the event of a tie for the grand winner, this shall be decided by a repeat of the Accuracy contest, but using right and left-handed boomerangs on alternate throws.*

General rules: *Each contestant furnishes his own boomerangs, which may be made of any desired material, but must be two-bladed, and free from auxiliary motors, rocket tubes, or the like, and must be thrown by bare hands, without the use of launching devices of any sort.*

All throws must be made in calm air, *hereby defined as being below 2.4 km/h (1.5 mph) as measured with an anemometer, approximately equivalent to conditions where a column of smoke from a cigarette will rise for 30 centimetres (one foot) without deviating more than 15 centimetres (six inches) from the vertical. In the event of windy weather, the contest shall be postponed until suitable conditions prevail. Throwing may be permitted in breezes of up to 4.8 km/h (3.0 mph) only with the unanimous consent of all registered contestants.*

The decisions of the judges are final unless shouted down by a really overwhelming majority of the crowd present. Abusive and obscene language may not be used by contestants when addressing members of the judging panel, or, conversely, by members of the judging panel when addressing contestants (unless struck by a boomerang).

Any underhanded trick or legalistic use of loopholes in these rules by a contestant to gain an unfair advantage over other contestants is expressly forbidden.

It is hoped by the M.C.E.R.A.B.T.A. that the above rules may serve as a useful standard set of rules for amateur boomerang throwing competitions throughout the Commonwealth of Australia and the rest of the civilised world where boomerangs are thrown.

SPECIAL 1974 AMENDMENT: The use of any string, wire or anything else attached from tip to tip of the boomerang as an aid in catching is forbidden.

Either the B.A.A. or M.C.E.R.A.B.T.A. is applicable to a large scale contest. But the best way to have an impromptu competition is to simply throw the boomerang, counting the number of steps that the thrower has to go to pick it up, subtracting one if he catches it. This may never decide a world title but it is good fun.

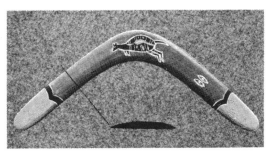

18 The late Bill Onus was probably the best-known Aborigine in Australia in his day, and easily the best boomerang maker. This boomerang was his best model and hence something pretty special. It is made of compacted red fibre, and decorated in Onus's characteristic style.
Wingspan 41.8 cm, **weight** 131 grams, **thickness** 5.1 mm, **range** 32 metres.

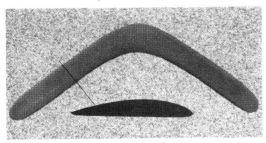

19 This high-impact polystyrene boomerang made by the Wham-O Co., USA, is probably the most popular boomerang in the world today and was the first plastic boomerang designed by one of the authors.

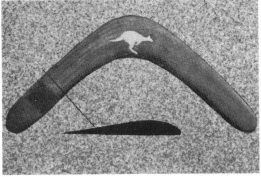

20 This small boomerang is the best plastic boomerang ever designed, combining wind resistance, short range and relative ease in throwing. With it one of the authors won a title at the 1973 National Championships in Canberra.
Wingspan 30.5 cm, **weight** 57 grams, **thickness** 4 1 mm, **range** 23 metres.

KEY TO COMPARATIVE SIZES

30 cm

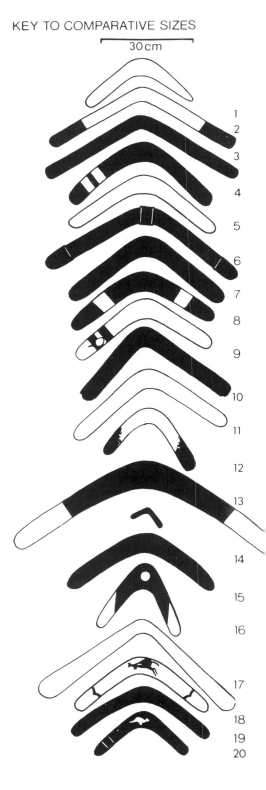

1
2
3
4
5
6
7
8
9
10
11
12
13
14
15
16
17
18
19
20

8.
BOOMERANG CONSTRUCTION

'Of acacia wood shall you make it.'
Exodus 30:1

Making a boomerang is not difficult—in fact it is a pleasant way to pass a few hours, being rewarded at the end with an interesting piece of sporting equipment which is uniquely one's own. Apart from time and patience, all one needs is a piece of suitable material, a good sharp knife, and some 80 or 120 grit garnet sandpaper. It is also a big help to have a couple of 'G' clamps for attaching the boomerang blank to a table or workbench while whittling away at it so as to be able to use both hands on the knife.

Fig. 25

The boomerang described in the following sections is an excellent one to construct, and if reasonable care is taken it should perform well and be a source of pleasure for many years. While it can be made from any medium density plywood, it is suggested that only marine or exterior grades should be employed, as these will tend to warp less should the boomerang be exposed to moisture. The plywood should be about 0.8 centimetres thick, and should be composed of five equal laminations. Apart from the superior strength of this material and its resistance to warping, the glue lines between laminae are a help in contouring the wing surface since they provide an easy visual guide to the depth of the cut.

The instructions are for a right-handed boomerang, but this need not deter left-handers: all that is necessary in their case is to view the relevant illustrations through a mirror and construct the mirror image boomerang instead.

Procedure

The simplest way to mark out the pattern of the boomerang onto the sheet of plywood is to cut out two strips of cardboard, each 23 centimetres long and 4.8 centimetres wide, as crude templates for the wings. These two strips of cardboard are put together at an angle of 110 degrees as shown in **Figure 26** and traced onto the plywood. The elbow curves are then drawn at a tangent to these lines using a 15 or 20 centimetre dinner plate. The resulting boomerang shape is then cut out with a fretsaw or bandsaw, and the ends rounded off smoothly using a large coin (a 20 cent piece is ideal) as a guide. The boomerang blank should then have the general outline shown in **Figure 27** which also illustrates the contours, or positions of the glue lines, of the finished boomerang.

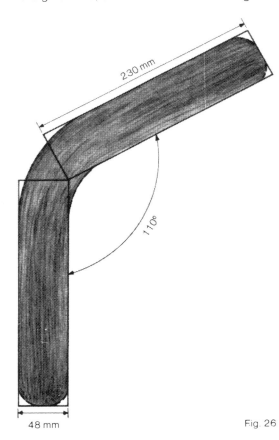

230 mm

110°

48 mm

Fig. 26

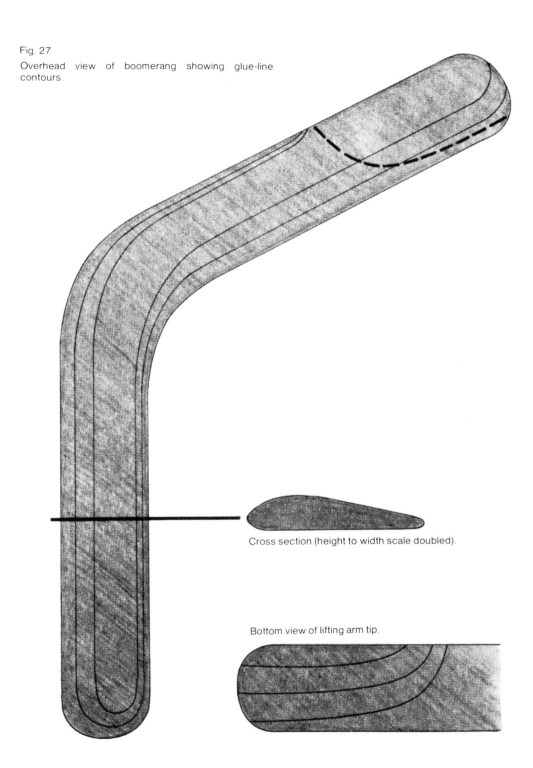

Fig. 27
Overhead view of boomerang showing glue-line
contours.

Cross section (height to width scale doubled).

Bottom view of lifting arm tip.

It is a good idea to have a whetstone handy when carving the boomerang, to keep the knife really sharp at all times. Nearly half of the material in the boomerang blank is going to be removed by the time the boomerang is finished, and if one has access to a belt sander, rasp, or the like in the early stages, so much the better. However, the final contouring should be done with a sharp knife to avoid irregularities.

When cutting through the outer veneers of the plywood, cuts in one direction may tend to rip the wood away jaggedly; in the other direction the cut will be smooth. Cutting strokes may therefore have to be made in one direction only for a given wing surface to avoid damage.

The object of the carving operation is to arrive at something like what is depicted in **Figure 27.** While it is not essential that the boomerang be exactly as shown, the closer the better, because this will reduce subsequent corrections made after test flying.

Weight is a matter of some concern at this stage. Weigh the boomerang on a set of postal balances to make sure that its weight is not more than 85 grams (three ounces). The arms of the boomerang need not be in perfect balance: when perched on a finger at the centre of the curve it is quite normal for the dingle arm to be heavier than the lifting arm (due to the bevelling of the latter on the under-surface), but it does not matter if the two arms are equal or even if the lifting arm is slightly the heavier, provided that sufficient material has been removed from its bevelled surface. However, it is important to check that the centre of rotation of the boomerang will be two to four centimetres away from the inside of the elbow curve. Do this by placing the boomerang on a flat table and pushing it slowly off so that the elbow goes over the table edge and then over-balances. The point at which the boomerang

Fig. 28

begins to overbalance should be within the inside of the elbow curve two to four cm past the table edge [7] **(Figure 28).**

Just as the proof of the pudding is in the eating, so the test of a boomerang is whether or not it will come back. A flight test is therefore essential, for if the boomerang needs adjustment, the only way to determine what corrections should be made is to throw it and note any deviations that occur. These deviations, and their corrections, are summarised below:

Boomerang faults due to mis-shaping
Fault (Figure 29)
Makes too wide a circuit.
Cause and remedy
Lift from bevel of lifting arm is insufficient. Cut the bevel more deeply so that it occupies a larger area and will 'bite' more air as it spins and hence tighten the circle.

Fault (Figure 30)
Spirals in too much and lands in front of the thrower.
Cause and remedy
Too much lift from the lifting arm. Add a layer of polyester putty or plastic wood to the bevel to reduce its effect.

[7]
When the boomerang is in flight there appears to be a 'hole' in the centre of the spinning outline of the boomerang. Some say that it is the motion of this hole that is important—the fact that it is surrounded by a spinning piece of wood is only of secondary interest!

(In Figure 29 to 35, the ideal flight path is shown in black and the faulty flight path dotted.

Fig. 29

Fault: Makes too wide a circuit.

Fig. 30

Fault: Spirals in too much and lands in front of the thrower.

Fig. 31

Fault: Steadily loses altitude on the return journey and crashes into the ground.

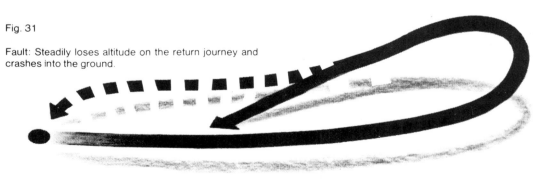

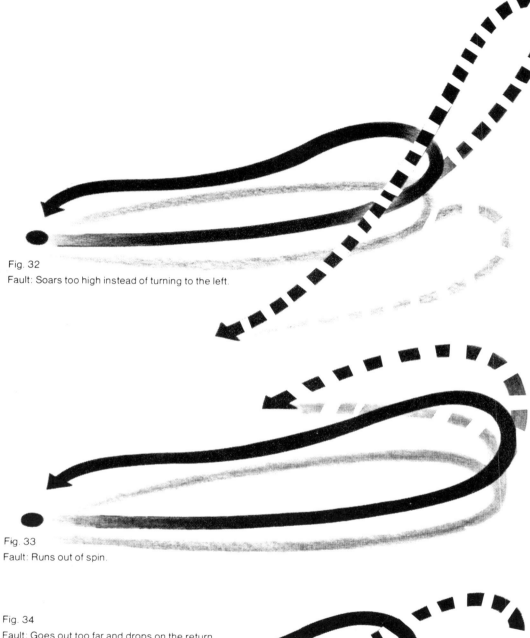

Fig. 32
Fault: Soars too high instead of turning to the left.

Fig. 33
Fault: Runs out of spin.

Fig. 34
Fault: Goes out too far and drops on the return

Fault (Figure 31)
Steadily loses altitude on the return journey and crashes into the ground.
Cause and remedy
Insufficient lift from the dingle arm. Undercut it lightly or sand the bottom of its leading edge so it will gain more uplift from below.

Fault (Figure 32)
Soars too high instead of turning to the left.
Cause and remedy
Insufficient lift on both arms: remove more material from the bevel and from all trailing edges so they are more deeply angled. Check that the boomerang is not warped.

Fault (Figure 33)
Runs out of spin.
Cause and remedy
Blunt leading edges, especially on the tip of the dingle arm. Use a bit more sandpaper to streamline it more.

Fault (Figure 34)
Goes out too far and drops on the return.
Cause and remedy
Too heavy. Take a bit off all surfaces in proportion.

Fault (Figure 35)
Has a flight path like the letter S instead of the letter O.

Cause and remedy
Insufficient lift on lifting arm and too much lift on dingle arm. Increase the cut of the lifting arm bevel.

Basically there is nothing complicated about adjusting the relative lifts from each wing to give a satisfactory flight. Cutting a wing surface to increase the amount of angled cut on surfaces A and D will increase the lift, while increasing the angled surface on B will decrease the lift. Normally surface C is left alone.

Fig. 36

Remember that no two boomerangs have exactly the same flight characteristics; it may be necessary to adjust one's throwing technique slightly to adapt to a particular boomerang. If the boomerang is capable of an exact return without wind assistance it is, by definition, a success; the fact that it throws differently from some other boom-

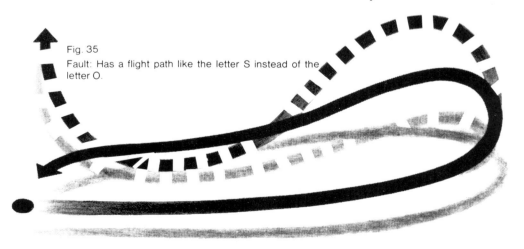

Fig. 35

Fault: Has a flight path like the letter S instead of the letter O.

erang is immaterial. After all adjustments have been completed, the boomerang should be coated with a paraffin or silicone-based wax to protect it from moisture and to reduce air friction.

The effects of warping

Up to this point all discussion of the aerodynamic forces acting upon a boomerang has assumed that the boomerang is essentially flat. In practice there may be some departure from this ideal, for most substances bend or distort to some extent in time. Wood especially is prone to absorb or release moisture, depending upon the relative humidity of the air, with a resulting expansion or contraction. If there is unevenness in the structure of the wood, there will be a tendency to warp — particularly with a boomerang carved from a section of bent root or branch. The usual procedure in commercial boomerang manufacture is to slice up the root or branch with a bandsaw. As a result all sections except the centre one will be very susceptible to warping.

A warped boomerang looks a little peculiar, of course, but the effects of warping on the boomerang's flight are evident long before one can even begin to notice that the boomerang is not as it should be. A boomerang which warps so that its 'flat' side is in fact slightly concave will have a longer than normal range, and will tend to crash into the ground before completing its return. If it can be thrown leaned over at a flatter than normal angle, and made to return, it will nevertheless be incapable of hovering satisfactorily. Warp in the opposite direction,

so that the 'flat' side is slightly convex, is not as serious (unless it is extensive) and can usually be corrected in throwing by holding the boomerang more upright than normal, and by throwing it more gently. This type of warping causes the boomerang to spiral upward, and reduces the range **(Figure 37)**.

The anti-warp boomerang splice

Not all types of wood are available in the convenient form of laminated sheets, and in making a boomerang it is sometimes necessary to start off with a straight piece of timber. Conversion of this to a boomerang blank is not difficult, and in the process it is possible to compensate for any future warping that might occur. The steps in this procedure are illustrated in **Figure 38.**

Take a piece of suitable timber about two centimetres thick, five centimetres wide and 30 centimetres long. Cut it carefully in half through the two centimetres dimension. Turn one of the pieces upside down in relation to the other, and put them together at the desired angle and mark it accordingly. Make a neat cut halfway through each piece where marked, using a fine-toothed hacksaw, and cut or chisel away the unwanted segment so the remaining pieces can be mortised together with a flush fit. Glue the two pieces together, then draw a curve at a tangent to the two arms (as with the plywood model) on the outside of the elbow curve. Carefully cut the little triangular piece away from its original position and glue it to the inside of the elbow curve, where it should fit exactly and act as a brace to relieve the stress on the elbow join during a rough landing.

It is hard to say whether the resulting boomerang should be regarded as made from a single piece of wood (which it was originally) or from four pieces (as in the final assembly)—but it has the advantage of being pretty well unaffected by warping, for anything which causes one arm to bend in one direction should cause the other arm to bend in the opposite direction to the same extent, thus cancelling, for all practical purposes, the effect upon the flight.

Fig. 37

A boomerang which warps so that its flat side is convex will have extra lift and a reduced range.

A boomerang which warps so that its flat side is concave will usually fly poorly and crash into the ground.

(In this diagram the flat side is facing downward.)

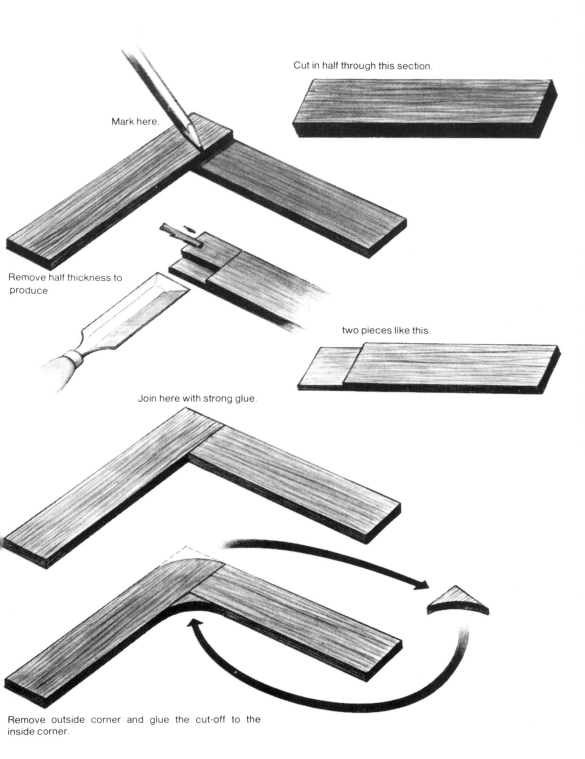

Cut in half through this section.

Mark here.

Remove half thickness to
produce

two pieces like this.

Join here with strong glue.

Remove outside corner and glue the cut-off to the
inside corner.

Fig. 38

Materials

While a boomerang can in theory be fashioned from almost any solid material, few can surpass the traditional one—wood. This is not to imply that there is no place in the making of boomerangs for other substantances — far from it! But for most practical boomerangs, a wood which is tough, well seasoned, and which has a specific gravity of about 0.8 is hard to surpass.

Over the course of many years the authors have fashioned boomerangs not only from various types of wood, but from other substances as well. Some of these worked very well, others very badly. Others were excellent in limited ways. Brief summaries follow of the uses of these various substances.

Acacia wood Of the many species of acacia growing in Australia the roots of the black wattle **(Acacia mearnsi)** have been highly prized for centuries as being suitable for boomerangs. Happily they have almost no tendency to warp, and grow away from the trunk of the tree at an angle of from 100 degrees to 120 degrees, so that the grain of the wood is about right for boomerangs. A second species of wattle, **A. aneura** or mulga, is used widely for the mass production of ornamental 'non boomerangs' because of its attractive appearance. Unfortunately it is one of the hardest woods in the world, being impossible to cut with a knife, and one of the few woods which is so dense that it sinks in water.

Californian redwood This low density wood (specific gravity 0.4) is excellent for making ultra-light boomerangs capable of going around twice in circles nearly the same size. Boomerangs made of this wood 'float' through the air, hover beautifully, and are extrernely easy for beginners to throw. Unfortunately the wood is rather weak and brittle, and boomerangs made from it tend to fracture on impact.

Silky oak (Grevillea robusta) This timber is interesting because its grain grows in two directions at once (at right angles to one another) with a beautiful structure known as a medullary ray. This makes it very resistant to splitting. All in all it is probably the best wood available for boomerangs, its chief disadvantage being its scarcity in Australia and general non-availability elsewhere.

Willow This is an excellent natural timber for boomerangs, having a good combination of toughness, lightness, and stability. It is preferred over all other woods, by many of Australia's best throwers and is available almost everywhere in the world.

Laminated woods By far the best all-round material for the construction of boomerangs. Unfortunately there is a tendency among manufacturers of plywoods to use rubbishy and inferior woods for the interior layers, finishing off with thin veneers of a showy wood on the outside, on the assumption that nobody is going to find out what the interior is like anyway. This is alright for most uses to which their products are put, such as panelling a wall or making a hen house, but it is not good enough for boomerangs. Any defects in internal construction become painfully apparent after portions of the outside layers have been removed, calling for tedious repairs before construction can proceed. The best policy when buying plywood for boomerang construction is to seek **exterior** or **marine grade** five-ply, looking closely at the edges to see that all laminations are the same thickness and that there are no gaps or cracks. All layers should be of the same type of wood, and the sheet should not be warped, as this would be an omen for future misery.

Price should not be a consideration when buying plywood for boomerangs, as there will be at the most only a few cents' difference in the cost of a boomerang made from the cheapest plywood and one made from the most expensive — which would be a short-sighted economy in view of the time that will be spent in shaping it.

Aircraft alloy Lightweight aluminium-magnesium alloys have been used successfully in making all-metal boomerangs by cutting out the basic shape with tin snips and then hammering out the curved aerofoil surfaces on an anvil. Boomerangs made in this

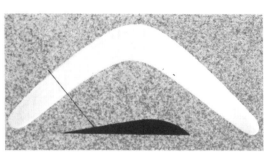

1 This boomerang was cut from plexiglass or perspex plastic, and its fast spinning and wind-resisting properties in flight led to refinements in the design of its successors.
Wingspan 36.2 cm, **weight** 94 grams, **thickness** 5.4 mm, **range** 29 metres.

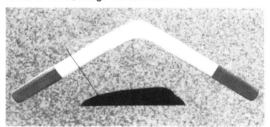

2 This nylon boomerang is made by W. Urban, Germany, and has a moderately long range. The aerofoil surfaces are angular instead of being rounded, which adds an air of excitement to any attempts to catch the thing unless gloves are worn or a finger-transplant surgeon is standing by.
Wingspan 57.8 cm, **weight** 160 grams, **thickness** 9.1 mm, **range** 33 metres.

3 This boomerang was made from whalebone by the late Frank Donnellan, and with it he made his terrific long distance throws. It is a little disappointing in calm air because it glides up and down a steep (45 degrees) flight path and swoops down in a wide freewheeling arc which is terrifying to anyone in the vicinity. In Frank's powerful hands, under appropriate wind conditions, it was most impressive, and its distance figures speak for themselves.
Wingspan 60.4 cm, **weight** 182 grams, **thickness** 5.2 mm, **range** up to 55 metres.

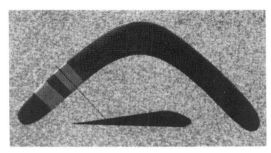

4 Five Australian ha'pennies are embedded in this boomerang—two in each wingtip and one at the elbow. Spins beautifully and has good range and hovering ability.
Wingspan 44.5 cm, **weight** 130 grams, **thickness** 9 mm, **range** 41 metres.

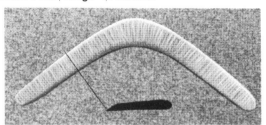

5 For many years this was the favourite boomerang of one of the authors and was given to him by the late Bill Onus of Belgrave, Victoria. Bill's boomerangs had an interesting cross section in that the upper surfaces of both arms were mirror symmetrical. This way the boomerang could be almost completed before one decided whether it was to be right-handed or left-handed; bevels undercut on the two under-surfaces determined this.
Wingspan 48.3 cm, **weight** 100 grams, **thickness** 7.3 mm, **range** 22 metres.

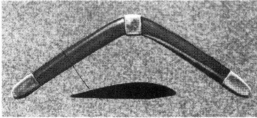

6 A distance boomerang made of laminated Queensland maple with copper-sheathed tips for greater weight and a higher moment of inertia. The dingle arm is undercut for its entire length with a bevel almost as deep as the one on the tip of the lifting arm.
Wingspan 61 cm, **weight** 155 grams, **thickness** 6.7 mm, **range** 45.7 metres.

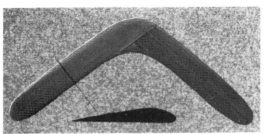

7 Made of spliced silky oak. Very satisfying to throw and quite reliable. A handy boomerang for exhibition throwing since it usually recovers well from a sloppy throw and hovers well for catching.
Wingspan 44.4 cm, **weight** 82 grams, **thickness** 7.1 mm, **range** 16.5 metres.

8 Of many hundreds of fibreglass boomerangs made in the same mould, this was the best and rivals similar ones made of plywood in its general performance. A bit painful to catch (if done incorrectly) because of its thinness.
Wingspan 40.5 cm, **weight** 101 grams, **thickness** 3.8 mm, **range** 21 metres.

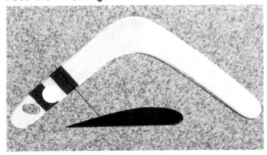

9 Made of spliced silky oak, this boomerang was inspired by a design feature originally used in an America's Cup yacht race some years ago when a small auxiliary rudder was incorporated for easy fine adjustment and trim. In the case of the boomerang this is accomplished by a small circular disc soldered to one end of a short copper wire (about a millimetre thick). The other end of the wire is embedded in a small hole in the boomerang wing. By leaving the disc parallel to the wing there is no effect, but by tilting it one way or another very fine adjustments can be made.

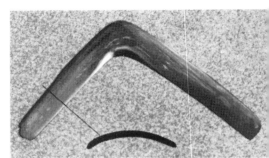

10 Made by D. Gibbons (England), this is the best all-metal boomerang to have come to the authors' attention. It makes a wide circuit, and spirals in to the thrower at the end. Not recommended for catching.
Wingspan 43.2 cm, **weight** 90 grams, **thickness** 1.2 mm, **range** 18.3 metres.

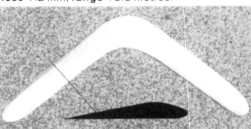

11 Spliced redwood was used for this boomerang, which has an unrivalled flight with regard to levelness and hovering at the end.
Wingspan 45.1 cm, **weight** 65 grams, **thickness** 7.5 mm, **range** 12 metres.

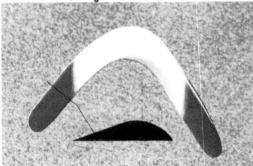

12 A King Billy hook boomerang made by B. Read, Wycheproof, Victoria. This little boomerang is very easy to throw, and has a fantastically level flight with unparalleled retention of spin. It will be noted that the lifting arm is the longer of the two. The upper surfaces are very deeply carved, with very little material being removed from the under side of the lifting arm.
Wingspan 30.5 cm, **weight** 75 grams, **thickness** 7.8 mm, **range** 37.5 metres.

way are very thin and make an interesting whistling noise as they spin through the air. They sound slightly dangerous—they are!

Fibreglass Except when used in very thin sections, fibreglass is a disappointment when used for making boomerangs. It is far too dense, and adds more to the weight than to the performance. It is not sufficiently strong for the purpose either, cracking badly on impact. It does have an application however in reinforcing the tips and elbows of wooden boomerangs, simultaneously increasing the moment of inertia and offering protection against abrasion.

Nylon This material can be injection-moulded at high temperatures and is well suited for the mass production of longer-range boomerangs. It is extremely tough and suffers practically no distortion on impact.

Polyethylene and Polypropylene These two plastics are the most woodlike in terms of their specific gravities, and can be used readily for the manufacture of boomerangs by injection moulding. Of the two, polyehtylene has a slightly lower s.g. and might be expected to produce a superior boomerang—however it bends on impact and always seems to have a slightly greasy feel about it so that it tends to slip out of the hand prematurely. Polypropylene is the most desirable plastic at present available for boomerangs because it is resilient and utterly unbreakable.

A.B.S. and High-Impact Polystyrene These plastics are tough and are used in many parts of the world for the moulding of boomerangs. High-impact polystyrene has the distressing characteristic of brittleness when cold, and should not be used for boomerangs that are going to be thrown in the winter. A.B.S. plastic is extremely tough at all temperatures. It is available in a range of densities through the use of varying amounts of a foaming agent which causes microscopic air bubbles to form at the time of moulding. Using this technique it is possible to obtain specific gravities very nearly as low as those for polyethylene.

Whalebone The late Frank Donnellan favoured this unusual material and used it, and similar related substances, for his long range boomerangs. He was not only the first to use it in a big way, but probably the last.

Red Fibre This pliant and durable material, available in large sheets and commonly used for making plumbing washers, was used extensively and with great success by the late Bill Onus for three of his commercial models. Today an Onus 'medium fibre boomerang' is a collector's item in great demand.

Because it is pliable, a boomerang made from this material can be bent to conform to the preferences of a particular thrower, and has, like a modern aeroplane propeller, a 'variable pitch'. Unfortunately it tends to distort and warp, and few throwers have the know-how or the strength to bend it back properly.

Bakelite impregnated cloth This material is commonly used for electrical insulating boards, and is fantastically tough and unbendable. Though rather heavy for general use, long range or wind-resistant boomerangs made from it fly well and are virtually indestructible.

Specialised boomerangs for special effects

The boomerang described on page 52 is probably one of the best ever devised. It is easy to throw, nice to watch, and can be made quite easily by a beginner. As with any boomerang, however, its variety of effects is limited and fairly specific to the boomerang. In order to extend the scope and range of one's throw, as well as one's skill as a craftsman and designer, one can modify this basic design and make up a set of specialised boomerangs such as those described below.

Figure eighter A basic wing breadth of 5.7 centimetres is used, with the tips basically elliptical in outline rather than rectangular—otherwise the dimensions of the basic boomerang remain unaltered. After shaping and before flight testing, however, cement strips of lead metal into the wing tips

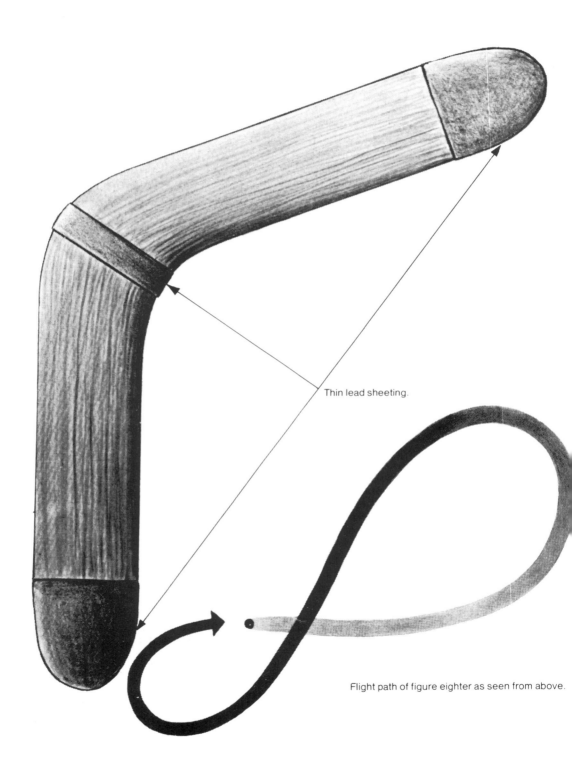

Thin lead sheeting.

Flight path of figure eighter as seen from above.

Fig. 39

and elbow, fitting flushly with the upper wing surfaces, to bring the total weight of the boomerang to 113 grams (four ounces). About one fifth of the added weight is in the elbow, the balance being distributed equally between the two wings. In flight the boomerang should come back past the thrower and then swing in again, with a flight path resembling a figure eight.

Long range In this case the widths of the wings of the basic model are unaltered but their lengths are extended to an overall span of 58 centimetres, with the dingle arm being about 2.5 centimetres longer than the lifting arm.

The bevelling on the underside of the lifting arm is the same as usual, but the entire under-surface of the dingle arm, from elbow to tip, is bevelled to the same extent. Cement thin sheets of lead or annealed copper to the upper surfaces of the wing tips and elbow to bring the total weight of the boomerang to approximately 127 grams (4½ ounces). As in the previous case, about a fifth of this added weight should go to the elbow, the rest to the wing tips in equal amounts. The range of this type of boomerang should be about 45 metres in still air and, within limits, the harder it is thrown the farther it will go (most other types have a fairly definite range). This boomerang maintains a remarkably level flight path: the throw made in front of Parliament House, Canberra, and illustrated on page 21 used this type of boomerang.

An interesting point about 'long distance' boomerangs: the distance a given boomerang **appears** to go depends almost as much upon what colour it is painted as upon its aerodynamics. A boomerang painted a light colour will appear to go further than a dark one. Painting boomerangs white seems to add an extra 10 metres to the range!

Twice arounder The basic boomerang is constructed of redwood or balsa. Balsa models should be coated with polyester resin to bring the final weight to approximately 50 grams (1¾ ounces). In throwing, the boomerang is aimed slightly higher than normal and thrown with a lot of spin. It should describe two circles of approximately equal size before finally spiralling in to the thrower (see **Figure 41**).

Fig. 40
Long range boomerang.

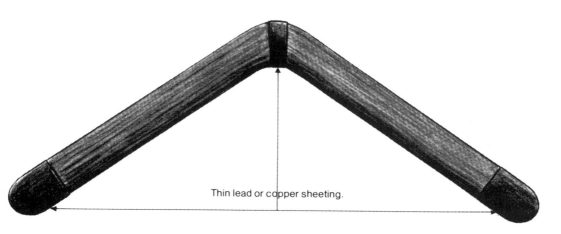

Thin lead or copper sheeting.

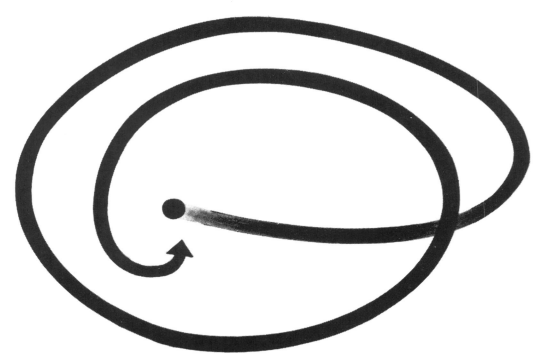

Fig. 41
Flight path of twice arounder as seen from above.

Windmaster By using a heavier material to keep the weight at about 85 grams (three ounces) while reducing the wingspan to 43 centimetres, it is possible to construct an extraordinarily stable boomerang which is relatively unaffected by winds that would blow larger or lighter boomerangs all over the place. This stability is due in part to the smaller area offered to the wind and partly to the increased rate of spin.

Whistler Almost any boomerang can be made to whistle as it flies through the air. Drill a hole in the wingtip and cement into it an empty .22 calibre long rifle cartridge so that the hollow rim protrudes slightly. It is preferable to do this on the opposite end to that by which the boomerang is held, so as not to cut the fingers when throwing. The sound generated by such a boomerang is most impressive.

Care and maintenance

Boomerangs should be lightly waxed after each throwing session (especially if thrown in moist grass) and then polished up immediately before being used again. Any chips or cracks should be repaired without delay and the new surfaces smoothed to blend with the original ones.

Excessive heat, dryness, and moisture should be avoided and boomerangs should never be carried or left on the rear deck or dashboard of a car. An ideal way to store a boomerang between uses is to attach it with rubber bands or light clamps to a similar sized boomerang blank.

Fig. 42
Protective anti-warp press.

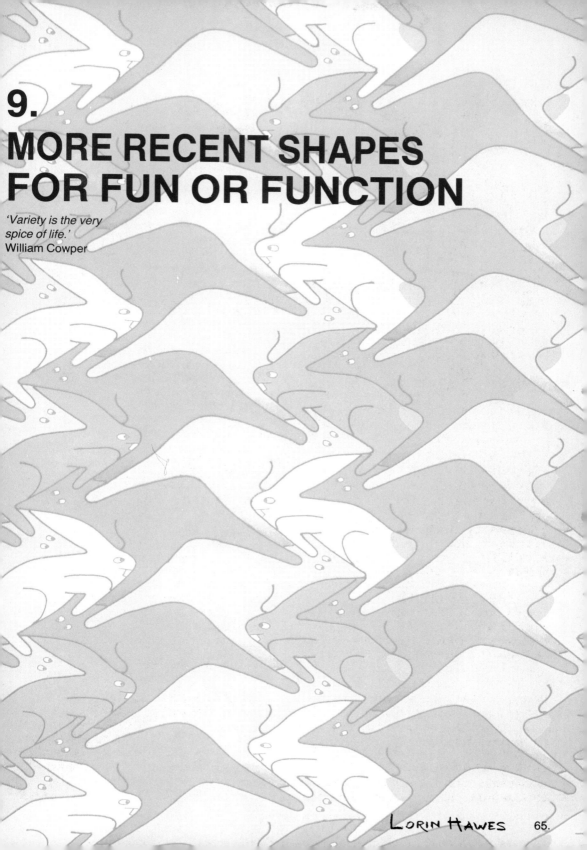

9.
MORE RECENT SHAPES
FOR FUN OR FUNCTION

*'Variety is the very
spice of life.'*
William Cowper

Recent shapes: for fun or function

Traditionally, the boomerang has a distinctive shape: two approximately equal arms at an angle somewhere between 90° and 130°, give or take a bit. Though this configuration still remains the most popular, modern curiosity and inventiveness have spawned a new generation of shapes. Some are designed to give their throwers an advantage in a particular type of competition — others are made for the sheer fun of having an unusually shaped object hurtle across the sky back to the thrower. Tomahawks, straight razors, kangaroos, triangles and even tennis racquets are among some of the shapes which have been made and which return to the thrower using the boomerang principle... as well as most numerals and letters of the alphabet!

Whether or not any or all of these should be called **boomerangs** is a point for debate, often quite heated, among enthusiasts.

To an anthropologist, any native artifact shaped like a boomerang is a boomerang, whether it returns or not. To some others, it is anything which returns, using the boomerang principle, regardless of shape or number of blades.

Quibbles of this nature are interesting but do not detract or modify the definition presented earlier of what a boomerang is (a boomerang-shaped object that boomerangs back to the thrower) indeed, if one simply calls anything returning by means of the boomerang principle a **"rang"** then a remarkable unity of common usage and definition is the result.

Without doubt the chief stimulus for proliferation in boomerang shapes, sizes and designs has been, in recent years, a general agreement on competitive events within boomerang associations of the world. Knowing how a given event is to be played created new interest in boomerang shapes, not for curiosity's sake, but rather to gain a competitive advantage in these newly defined competitions. Unlike other sports such as football or baseball which have the dimensions of the equipment specified precisely, boomerang competitors have the freedom to select (or, more often, to make) the instrument they will use in a particular competition.

A good thrower may do badly in a particular event if his boomerang is less suited to it than someone else's. Thus the design of a boomerang to perform best in each event of a given competition becomes at least as important as the skill and expertise involved in throwing.

While one could think up almost an infinite number of different competitive events, those accepted by serious throwers world wide are few: about a dozen or less. Most of these require both physical and intellectual skill, and virtually all require accuracy of return and a catch.

Perhaps the best known of the internationally recognised competitive events is that which is appropriately called the **Australian Round.** This event requires each competitor to launch the boomerang from the centre of a series of concentric circles drawn on the field. The closer that the boomerang returns to the centre, the more points the competitor receives. Additional points are earned if the boomerang is caught in midair, and/or if the boomerang travels outward past a defined distance (this calls for a line judge with cool nerves to stand close to the boomerang's orbit). Thus the total number of points gained on a given throw is based upon accuracy of return, whether it is caught, and how far it has gone. At the conclusion of a given number of throws, the points earned for each thrower are tabulated and the winner declared.

This competition led to the development of the Omega and the V-shape, for the idea is to have a small, easily caught boomerang that travels outward to the prescribed distance (but not much beyond it) while returning accurately with a bit of hover to permit the thrower enough time to get under it for an accurate catch.

In the **Accuracy** event, things are more simple as the boomerang is thrown from the centre of the circle as before, but this time no attempt is made to catch it. No extra points are awarded for the boomerang travelling extra distance, and scoring is easy: the competitor whose boomerang comes to rest closest to the centre is the winner!

Since no catch is required almost any shape and size of boomerang may be used. Weights are sometimes added to the centre of each arm to reduce hover so that the boomerang will not be blown away at the last minute by any breeze.

Fast Catch is an event requiring both speed and accuracy. This competition calls for five consecutive throws and catches. The boomerang must be thrown each time from within a small circle but may be caught outside of it. The competitor requiring the least time to complete five consecutive catches is the winner.

The boomerang for this event is usually small and V-shaped for ease in catching, and shaped with more than average lift to maintain a short range and quick turn-around. Weights are usually added to the centre of both arms to eliminate hover.

Juggling involves the alternate throwing and catching of two boomerangs so that at least one is in the air at all times, launching first one, then — as it is about to return and be caught, — the other. And so on, ad infinitum or until the thrower misses a catch. Scoring is based upon the total number of consecutive catches.

A pair of boomerangs well matched in flight characteristics and which hover well at the end are desired for this event. V-shaped boomerangs with flared tips are popular.

Doubling on the other hand, requires the competitor to launch two boomerangs simultaneously, catch each, and repeat the procedure until a boomerang is not caught and touches the ground.

For this event, the competitor prefers one boomerang which is short ranged and comes in quickly without hovering too much. The other boomerang circumscribes a larger circle and has substantial hover to give the thrower ample opportunity to get to it.

Maximum Time Aloft (MTA) is an event in which the boomerang is launched with the object of keeping it aloft for the longest time, then catching it before it hits the ground. There may or may not be restrictions on how far from the launch point the catch may be taken to be valid. In the "unlimited" case this may be hundreds of metres with the thrower in a desperate cross-country run trying to keep in touch so as to be able to catch the thing when it comes down. A strange twist to the concept of boomerang throwing for in this case it is the thrower who reunites with the boomerang rather than vice-versa!

Design characteristics for this event require that the boomerang makes a hasty turn about, very quickly coming into a hover, then retaining its spin as it slowly descends through auto-rotation, like a maple seed. Typically the boomerang is launched up very high for maximum effect.

A boomerang designed for this event is thin, light, and generally has the two arms about the same width and thickness, but of greatly different length, the dingle arm being about half the length of the other. The elbow angle is generally about 90°.

In conclusion:— it is not likely that boomerang shapes have reached the apex of design. As more and more people of an intelligent and inquisitive nature discover boomerangs, some of them will experiment, and from this will emerge other designs and other avenues of exploration.

Who knows? Perhaps you, dear reader may be the next to unlock another door in this magical world of the boomerang.

Contemporary Records and Achievements

For the sake of completeness — and by way of contrast with those listed previously, some of the recent records in boomerang throwing are listed below:—

Long Distance 145 metres by Volker Behrens of West Germany, March 1987.

Consecutive Catch (using two hands) 653, by Rob Kroll, Mt. Waverley, Victoria April 1985.

Juggling 68 consecutive catches by Bob Burwell of Brisbane Queensland. Set during the USBA National Championships June 1982.

Fast Catch Five throws and catches in 18.7 seconds by John Flynn of London, New Hampshire August 1985.

Doubling 29½ double catches by Chet Snouffer of Delaware Ohio August 1986.

Maximum Time Aloft (catch anywhere) 2 minutes 59.94 seconds by Dennis Joyce of Newport News, Virginia June 1987.

The Three Sigma boomerang pattern

The idea for this shape of boomerang came when observing the shape of the Gaussian curve of normal probabilities used in statistics. If you draw a line through the centre of the pattern it will illustrate the ordinates of the 'normal curve' as it is called. In statistical jargon, 3 sigma is the point near either end of the curve.

The scale of the illustration is half size hence double all dimensions when sketching it out onto graph paper, then cut the boomerang out on a rectangular piece of 6mm or quarter inch ply, 300 400mm. Five lamination birch or wood of similar specific gravity (about .4) is desirable.

Next, use a couple of pieces of scrap wood and a mirror to check the boomerang blank for warp, as indicated in Chapter 8. If the ends of the arms are warped downward, simply flip the blank over so that they turn upward instead and make that the topside. It is best of course to have the boomerang reasonably flat. Bend gently if necessary.

This pattern is for a right handed boomerang. To make it left handed, after cutting out the blank, place the pattern over a light and trace the contouring lines onto the reverse side of the pattern and follow these.

Alternatively, view the pattern in a mirror from this stage onward, and construct the mirror image boomerang.

Both arms have airfoils that face in the same direction, as you can see from the pattern. Shape the arms as indicated on the pattern with a sharp knife, rasp, or belt sander. Do the undercuts of the underside first. Then shape the top side taking care to blend gradually to the slightly different shape of the elbow.

When you are satisfied that you have shaped the boomerang correctly, first sand it with medium grit sandpaper, then with a fine grade until it is smooth throughout. The final weight should be close to 60 grams, or two ounces.

Take it to a large, open grassy field and give it a few flings in calm air. If the boomerang performs well — you've got it! If not, follow the tuning instructions in Chapter 8 and keep at it until you've got it right. Then sign it and date it because it probably won't be the last boomerang you'll make.

Seal the surface with lacquer or polyurethane: this adds gloss and helps it perform better in the air and look better in your hands.

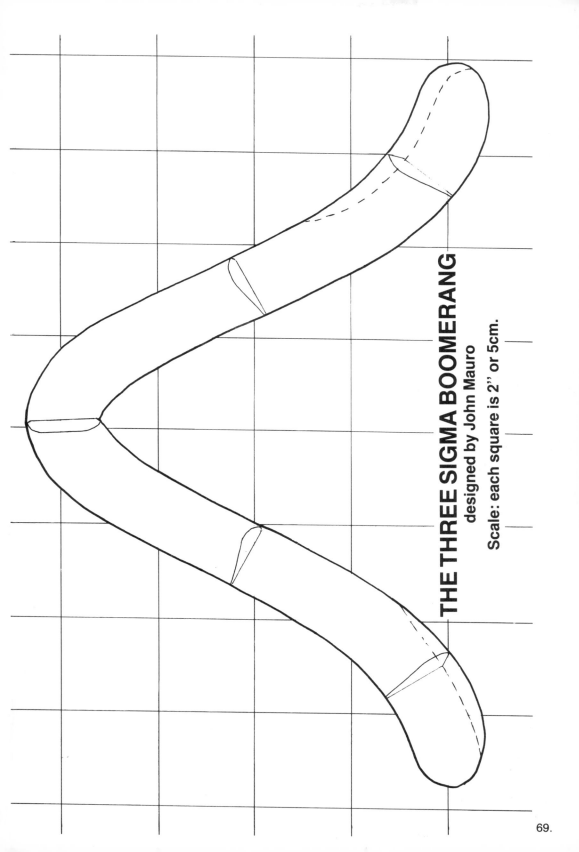

THE THREE SIGMA BOOMERANG

designed by John Mauro

Scale: each square is 2" or 5cm.

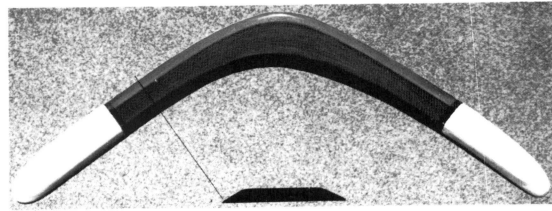

13 This incredible big boomerang was made and given to the authors by a fire-eater and magician in a circus which travelled through southern Queensland in 1971. It works surprisingly well as it spins its way through the air. If you, the reader, are that fire-eating magician, please get in touch with us so we can give better credit in future editions for your gigantic boomerang.

Wingspan 81.3 cm, **weight** 291 grams, **thickness** 9.8mm, range 22.8 metres.

14 The smallest and lightest boomerang that flies a perfect course. Made by Bevan Rayner of Bundeena, NSW, it is launched from the spring-loaded arm of a 15.2 cm high figure of an Aboriginal hunter, and lands in a little container at his feet.

Wingspan 10.8 cm, **weight** 0.4 grams, **thickness** 2.1 mm, **range** 1.8 metres.

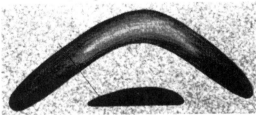

15 Victorian mountain ash was used in the major construction of this boomerang, which was then sheathed completely with fibreglass.

Wingspan 41.8 cm, **weight** 150 grams, **thickness** 10.1 mm, **range** 25.6 metres.

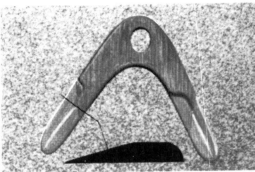

16 This boomerang is interesting for two reasons: the acute elbow angle and the fact that the entire aerodynamic action derives from the upper surface only, for the bottom is completely flat. Made by H. Boys, Kansas, USA.

Wingspan 27.3 cm, **weight** 56 grams, **thickness** 6.3 mm, **range** 16.5 metres.

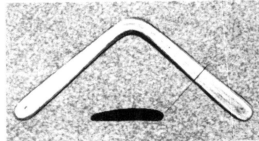

17 This boomerang was made by the Burwell brothers of Slacks Creek, Queensland, probably the leading constructors and throwers of novel boomerangs in the world. The inverse taper of the arms has obvious advantages in increasing the moment of inertia of the boomerang, eliminating the need for metal sheathing.

Wingspan 58.4 cm, **weight** 160 grams, **thickness** 9.1 mm, **range** 34.7 metres.

Questions & Answers

Being in the business of making and selling boomerangs and teaching people how to throw them, one gets the chance to answer lots of questions, sometimes silly, sometimes profound. Some are asked frequently, some seldom. Here's a selection of them:

Q. How can you tell if a boomerang will come back or not?

A. The only sure way is to throw it, for the differences between a good boomerang and a bad one are not immediately obvious, even to the expert eye. This is difficult of course when buying one; in this event it is wise to see if the maker had had the courage to put his name on it and his address on the instruction sheet.

Q. How can you tell when a boomerang is out of control?

A. The instant it leaves your hand.

Q. Isn't it unusual for a nuclear scientist to give up a life of University teaching and research to make boomerangs in the wilds of Queensland?

A. Yes.

Q. Did the ancient Aborigines make left handed boomerangs?

A. Yes — and in a higher proportion than we make today. In sorting through museum collections of boomerangs and kylies, the fraction of left handers is about one quarter, or roughly twice the fraction of left handers in the population today. Doubtless there was less pressure upon children, in a non-literate society, to conform to right handedness. The boomerang is probably unique among ancient artifacts in identifying whether its owner was right or left handed.

Q. How far can a boomerang be thrown?

A. If it is stipulated that the boomerang return to the throwing point, and if it is thrown under windless conditions and the ground distance measured with a tape rather than being estimated, the distance always seems to be less than 60 metres. Greater distances might be claimed but it is a good idea to be sceptical. Skilful liars outnumber skilful boomerang throwers by a wide margin!

Q. Do boomerangs go farther at higher altitudes?

A. Yes — and at an elevation of a mile the effect is dramatic. But even more striking is the loss of "quality" of boomerang flight for hovering effects disappear and a boomerang comes in like a dead duck. It is difficult to apply enough spin to a "sea level" boomerang for it to operate above this altitude. The reason is simple: while the air which supplies lift thins out a lot, the force of gravity remains about the same.

Q. Have I heard the joke about the Aborigine who was given a new boomerang and went crazy trying to throw his old one away?

A. No. Please tell it.

BOOMERANGS ON THE REAR COVER

in clockwise sequence, starting at upper right.

1. MTA boomerang by Ted Bailey, Ohio. Wingspan 380mm, weight 10 grams, stays aloft up to three minutes. Maybe more!

2. M-17 boomerang by Lorin Hawes of laminated hardwood from the Daintree rainforest, little changed from its 1959 ancestor. Wingspan 430mm, weight 60 grams, range about 20 metres.

3. Strip laminated boomerang by Al Gerhards, Pennsylvania. In this construction, wood is cut into thin strips, bent, glued together again, then shaped. Wingspan 447mm, weight 70 grams, range about 40 metres.

4. Silky Spinner boomerang by Lorin Hawes, using the technique described on page 57. Wingspan 428mm, weight 52 grams, range about 18 metres.

5. Superbly made boomerang by Ray Reiser, Pennsylvania using the plan shown in Chapter 8. Wingspan 410mm, weight 64 grams, range about 35 metres, (a bit longer than normal).

6. Sky Hawk boomerang by Dan Russell, California. Wingspan 387mm, weight 48 grams, range about 28 metres.

7. Hook type boomerang by Herb Smith, England. Wingspan 374mm, weight 85 grams, range about 30 metres.

8. Boomerang Fever by Barnaby Ruhe, Pennsylvania. Moulded from Polypropylene; wingspan 335mm, weight 45 grams, range about 30 metres.

9. Saxon Pacemaker fast catch. A V-shaped boomerang with flared tips by Thomas Hartman, West Germany. Wingspan 330mm, weight 32 grams, range about 20 metres.

10. Oregon Hat omega boomerang by Dough DuFresne, Oregon. Wingspan 335mm, weight 42 grams, range about 30 metres.

11. Prodigal by Bob Poole, Georgia. Wingspan 346mm, weight 65 grams A 'keyhole omega' made of laminated Baltic birch.

12. Reverse hook by Volker Behrens, West Germany. Incredibly fine strip laminations (about 80) are a feature of this boomerang. Wingspan 396mm, weight 50 grams, range about 30 metres.